LINCOLN AND CIVIL WAR POLITICS

LINCOLN AND CIVIL WAR POLITICS

Edited by JAMES A. RAWLEY

The University of Nebraska

Generously Donated to
The Frederick Douglass Institute
By Professor Jesse Moore
Fall 2000

HOLT, RINEHART AND WINSTON
New York • Chicago • San Francisco • Atlanta
Dallas • Montreal • Toronto • London • Sydney

Cover illustration: Abraham Lincoln. Photograph by Alexander Gardner, November 15, 1863. (*The Granger Collection*)

CONTENTS

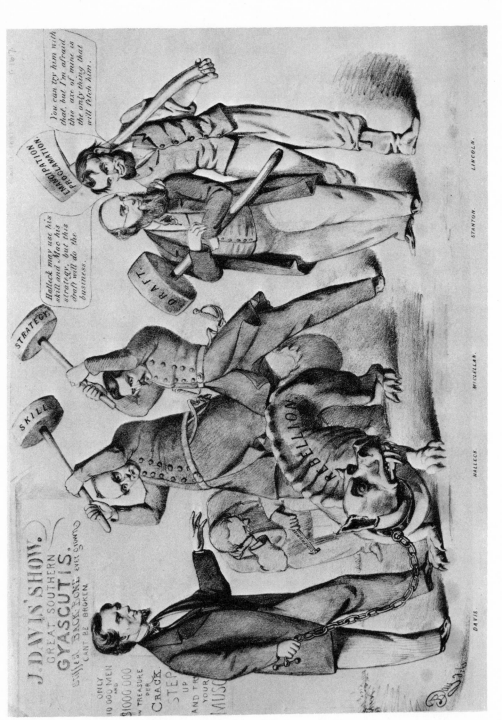

"Breaking that 'Backbone.'" Print by Currier & Ives, 1862. (*New York Public Library*)

INTRODUCTION

The Civil War, while deciding the survival of the Republic, challenged American political institutions, especially the Constitution, the Presidency, and the party system. The war was preceded by heated controversy over constitutional issues. In the decade before the war one major party had succumbed to political strife and a new one had been born. Weak presidents had acquiesced in policies that promoted crisis. Sectional antagonisms beset national unity. In 1861 the "more perfect Union," whose affairs were administered by political parties, ruptured. Bound up with the question of survival were problems touching upon constitutional and political issues of presidential power, personal liberty, congressional authority, party factionalism, political motivation, and the place of state and sectional interests within the national polity.

The Civil War offers an example of crisis government without parallel in United States history. The nearest analogy perhaps is the Great Depression. The war posed fundamental questions. How did a constitutional democracy—granted express powers by the governed—function in crisis? In what ways did crisis assail the frame of government? To what extent did regular procedure prevail? What role did the President assume? How did political patronage serve as a weapon during the war? What role did political parties play? What was the character of the dominant party? Of the minority party? Were the parties instruments of construction or obstruction? What were their motives? To put the root question, still partially unanswered by historians, what were the politics of the Civil War?

Civil War politics as a field of serious study has been little cultivated. As far as they have worked the field, historians have tended to concentrate on Lincoln, on the extremist, or Radical, members of the Republican party, on the allegedly treasonous Democrats—in short, on personalities, conflict, and disloyalty. Only in recent years, as the dates of the readings in this work demonstrate, have scholars begun to devote their efforts to understanding the politics of the war years with something of the same fullness that has been lavished upon study of the causes of the Civil War or of Reconstruction.

The war within the nation exerted an unexampled strain on the American political system. The administration party, being almost exclusively northern, had been a cause of disunion. The other major party, though now divided into northern and southern wings, had long ruled the nation, with strong support from the South. The administration party had several striking features besides its sectional character. It was new, formed only in the mid-fifties. It was invertebrate, being a coalition of old parties and a confederation of state Republican organizations. It had never enjoyed the spoils of office or the responsibilities of power. It had won victory on the issue of containing slavery, but immediately on coming into office it had found the major issue changed to saving the nation.

The Republican party needed clear leadership, coherence, and cooperation from the opposition. Though it had won the Presidency, it controlled Congress not through the electors' mandate but through the southerners' withdrawal. It did not control the Supreme Court, whose members were hostile to Republican doctrine. It suspected the loyalty of the opposition party. It administered a government struggling for its life, but confined by a written constitution and by custom.

The new party was committed by its platform to a new economy, but it was divided by an East-West sectionalism and by discordant views on slavery and confiscation. At once nationalistic and respectful of states' rights, it was constrained by circumstances to wield centralized power over state and citizen and to temper constitutional liberties because of wartime exigencies. Itself an untried instrument, it was compelled to test the functioning of the Presidency, the Congress, and the Supreme Court in an unpacific workshop preyed upon by folk fears of dictators, traitors, and miscegenationists.

Knit together only by the thin strand of antiextensionism, the party found itself impelled by the pressures of a war that was widely thought to be caused by slavery to move against slavery itself. Encompassing commercial and industrial as well as agrarian elements, the party sought to enact a neo-Hamiltonian program that benefited bankers, manufacturers, and railroad promoters as well as a limited neo-Jeffersonian program that benefited farmers, friends of education, and shippers.

The Democratic party, like the nation, was severed by secession. Not only did it lose its southern arm, but with the death of Stephen A. Douglas in June 1861 also its principal northern leader. The war suddenly made it a minority party. At first, in a surge of nationalism, it abundantly supported the majority party. But as Republican party strategists tried to merge the opposition into a party of the Union and as partisan editors tarred Democrats as Copperheads, Democrats, threatened with their own survival, found themselves increasingly called upon to assert their traditional principles.

They championed minimal national government, constitutional guarantees of individual liberties, the rights of states to control their own institutions, including slavery, and agrarian economics, and they were disinclined to share in a prevailing hatred of the South. Increasingly they criticized arbitrary government, emancipation, military failures, and subjugation of the South.

The selections reprinted here focus on three chief topics: the President, the congressional Republicans, and the Democrats. Two new directions of scholarly inquiry become apparent. One is the interpretive shift away from the older stress on conflict in politics to a stress on consensus. This shift is part of a broad trend in interpreting American history. Examples of both emphases, conflict and consensus, appear in the selections, in discussion of executive and legislature, President and Radicals, and Republicans and Democrats.

The other new direction is methodological. Traditional historical analysis of American political behavior has proved inadequate. Political historians have paid too little attention to quantitative techniques. They often have impressionistically generalized from literary materials, for example, speeches, newspapers, letters, and diaries. New research methods developed by academic disciplines other than history have opened new opportunities to make generalizations based on quantitative analysis. With punch cards and computers, scholars are able to collect and evaluate political data. The results can be presented in tabular form. This procedure may reveal more accurately than the older methods such determinants of political behavior as party, faction, and section.

Historians need to discover specifically how the American political system worked during the fiery trial of internal war. How far did Lincoln stretch the Constitution? What effects did the patronage system have on party and northern unity? What was the President's relationship with state political leaders? Did a Radical Republican faction at cross-purposes with the President over the aims and conduct of the war vigorously oppose and ultimately overwhelm Lincoln? Who were the Radicals? How unified a group were they? How did they actually vote? Were the Democrats treasonous "Copperheads" or members of the loyal opposition? Midwestern agrarians or Negrophobes? These are some of the questions examined in the following pages.

In a speech made in 1856 Lincoln asserted that the Constitution "must be maintained, for it is the only safeguard of our liberties." Some contemporaries and later critics accused him, however, of setting himself up as a dictator, encroaching upon congressional powers, seizing control of sword and purse, subverting personal liberties, and disregarding the Supreme Court. Trenchant criticism of these infractions appeared in the classic history of the Civil War by James Ford Rhodes, published 1895–1899. Lincoln's deeds between the fall of Fort Sumter and the convening of Congress in special session, Rhodes judges, were "the acts of a Tudor rather than those of a constitutional ruler." Rhodes was especially severe in indicting Lincoln for his violations of personal liberty through executive suspension of the privilege of habeas corpus, arbitrary arrests, and abridgments of freedom of speech and press. Through the method of comparative history he examined Lincoln's rigor during the Civil War and the British government's during the French Revolution, to the disadvantage of the American ruler.

Writing a generation later than Rhodes and after dictatorships had been established in Soviet Russia and Fascist Italy, James G. Randall offered an Olympian view of Lincoln's adherence to constitutional principles. In *Constitutional Problems Under Lincoln*, which appeared in 1926, Randall, also drawing upon comparative history, defines the American and British attitude toward the rule of law, scrutinizes

Lincoln's interpretation of the war power, and notes ambiguities in congressional and court actions. "A comparison with European examples," he concludes, "shows that Lincoln's government lacked many of the earmarks of dictatorial rule." The reader is left to decide for himself whether Lincoln was, as a Harvard law professor charged in 1862, "a monarch . . . a perfect military despotism."

By the time Lincoln acceded to the Presidency the spoils system was well entrenched. He headed a new party which included thousands of supporters hankering to hold office. To what ends was the patronage to be used? Did Lincoln abuse the appointment power, demeaning the civil service in order to distribute the spoils? Did he use the patronage for personal aggrandizement, with an eye to his own power and re-election? Or did he use it as the cement of party and Union? The selection from *Lincoln and the Patronage* (1943) by Harry J. Carman and Reinhard H. Luthin will help the student answer these questions. A foremost theme to hold in mind is the relevance of patronage to party politics and presidential leadership.

In 1861 the federal Union was still being described as "our confederacy." States' rights were a firm tradition in the North as well as in the South where the doctrine had justified secession. Similarly, the Republican party was a loose coalition of former Whigs, Free-Soilers, anti-Nebraska Democrats, and members of other factions. Its strength lay in state organizations, represented in a national executive committee.

William B. Hesseltine in "Abraham Lincoln and the Politicians" analyzes Lincoln's role in dealing with a decentralized party, controlled in 1860, he argues, by the governors and divided in Congress into factions headed by practiced politicians. The critical reader, who earlier has read that Lincoln was a dictator, may consider whether the governors dominated the party in 1860, how Lincoln prevailed over state organizations, in what degree his actions are better explained by political rather than military exigency, and whether—especially in the light of later selections—the Republican party was rent by states' rights and party factionalism. In *Lincoln and the War Governors,* published in 1948, Hesseltine sets forth in detail his view of how Lincoln triumphed over the governors and how through him the nation triumphed over the states.

The historiographical problem of the Radicals has led to one of the liveliest controversies among Civil War historians in recent years. When Congress convened in December 1861, following military reverses at Bull Run and Ball's Bluff, it formed a Joint Committee on the Conduct of the War. The committee functioned throughout the war, seeking and securing a share in control of military policy and in deciding questions of strategy and tactics.

Its extraconstitutional behavior, impinging upon the President's role as commander in chief, seemed to smack of factional politics. As the war dragged on, the committee tended toward extremeness. It became the agent of the Radicals, a faction within the Republican party which in general favored vigorous prosecution of the war, severe treatment of rebels, and drastic action against slavery. Lincoln was criticized by the Radicals with increasing acrimony.

T. Harry Williams in his lively *Lincoln and the Radicals,* written in a brilliant literary style and published in 1941, portrays the wartime leader pitted against extremists in his own party. Using conventional methods, Williams found the Radicals to be a distinct, cohesive group marked by their insistence upon immediate emancipation, their zeal for prosecution of the war, their intention to gain ascendancy in the party, and above all by their design to entrench industrial capitalism in the nation. In short, the Radicals, though a minority in the Republican ranks, were an identifiable, unified group animated by revolutionary social, political, and economic aims, which they ultimately imposed upon a beleaguered President. The Joint Committee on the Conduct of the War was the instrument "by which the radical faction hoped to direct the military struggle for the attainment of its own partisan ends."

A fresh evaluation of the Radicals appeared in 1964 from the pen of Hans L. Trefousse. His measured piece, "The Joint Committee on the Conduct of the War: A Reassessment," enumerates the committee's successes, questions its reputation as a court of star chamber, discovers Lincoln's use of the committee for constructive ends, acknowledges the committee's skill in spreading propaganda, and minimizes its influence. Focusing on the main Radical agency, Trefousse argues, "It simply did not possess the power to act."

The impact of quantitative analysis on the continuing dialogue about the Radicals may be seen in the contributions of Glenn M. Linden and Allan G. Bogue. Their work is significant for its methodology and conclusions. Drawing on his unpublished doctoral dissertation, Linden in 1967 presented his study, " 'Radicals' and Economic Policies: The House of Representatives, 1861–1873." After noting the discord produced by earlier methods, he sought greater precision by analysis of representatives' voting records. By testing a series of political measures, he identified a group of Radicals far larger and very different from men previously identified. He then examined the connection between political and economic Radicalism, seeking to test whether cohesion on political legislation carried over to economic legislation, as Williams had claimed. And finally, he raised the question whether representatives voted on economic issues along party or geographical lines. Linden's Radicals bear scant resemblance to those of Williams in personnel, unity, or motive.

Allan G. Bogue set out to understand major forces in congressional voting, asking in particular whether party or faction was the more significant influence on Republican voting. His methodology in quantification was more sophisticated than Linden's, and perhaps more precise. "Bloc and Party in the United States Senate, 1861–1863," published in 1967, concentrates on the upper chamber during the second session of the Thirty-seventh Congress, which passed a body of far-reaching economic measures. Carefully describing his procedure, he dissects aspects of sectional, factional, and party voting. Not completely overturning Williams, Bogue believes that in the Civil War Congress "a variety of determinants of political behavior were interacting."

That northern Democrats were treasonous was part of the Republican creed.

They bore the reproachful stamp Copperhead for their supposed sympathy for the South and opposition to the Lincoln administration. The Democratic party, once dominant in the United States, suffered for its wartime reputation long after the war, as Republican orators waved the "bloody shirt" of the "rebellion" to remind voters who had saved the Union. No general history of the wartime Democrats by a historian appeared before 1942, when Wood Gray's *The Hidden Civil War* was published. Even then the author did not dissociate himself far from the Copperhead tradition.

The Hidden Civil War remains the standard work. Gray was unable to discern much good in the party's leaders, whom he found to be narrow and prejudiced men, obstructionists and defeatists. Some of them formed secret societies and connived with Confederate agents. This movement, centering in the Middle West and pressing for a peace without victory, presented a danger to democracy.

Nearly a score of years later, Frank L. Klement, in *The Copperheads in the Middle West* (1960), provided a fresh analysis. Concentrating on the heartland of Copperheadism, resting his research more heavily on manuscripts than did Gray, who had used newspapers extensively, he arrived at opposing conclusions. The Copperheads, according to Klement, were loyal to the Union, sectional in outlook, and agrarian in philosophy. They were pro-western rather than pro-southern, anti-industrialist and anti-nationalist, deriving their views from Jeffersonian and Jacksonian backgrounds and anticipating Grangerism and Greenbackism.

The Northwest, where Copperheadism flourished, was investigated from another approach in 1963 by Jacque Voegeli. In his essay, "The Northwest and the Race Issue, 1861–1862," he departed from traditional concerns about loyalty, pacifism, and pro-southernism. Interested in both major parties, he gave abundant attention to the Republicans and the Northwest's influence in Congress. In his study of the region's politics culminating in the congressional elections of 1862, he stresses love neither for the Confederacy nor for agrarian economics behind the Democratic party's victories. The issue of slave emancipation played a leading role. Moreover, and most important, "This opposition to emancipation was primarily the product of Negrophobia aggravated by the threat of a massive influx of Negroes."

The studies by Gray, Klement, and Voegeli consider the Copperheads from national and regional vantage points, with little analysis of the Democratic party's record in Congress. This important side of the matter, the party's actual conduct in the Thirty-seventh Congress, was investigated in 1966 by Leonard P. Curry in "Congressional Democrats, 1861–1863." Curry examined both branches of Congress and, in keeping with recent trends in methodology, analyzed voting performance. His conclusions are striking. Congressional Democrats were loyal to the Union, and although leaderless after the death of Douglas, they maintained a surprising degree of party unity. They supported both the war effort and Republican nonwar measures. House Democrats tended to be more obstructionist than Senate members, but in general the party was not extremist or fractious. Congressional Democrats were conservatives, standing toward the political center. Their voting behavior suggests not dissension but a northern consensus.

Clearly, historians will continue to study the politics of the Civil War. Possibly the work has just begun; certainly it is moving in new directions. The partisanship and hysteria that metamorphosed Lincoln into a dictator, his Republican disputants into Radicals and Jacobins, and Democrats into Copperheads seem to have dissipated. A new interpretation of American history aware of consensus as well as of conflict, a new methodology using quantification as well as conventional records, a wider perception employing interdisciplinary research, and a more realistic understanding of politics and human nature based respectively upon a more thorough knowledge of the American political process and of modern psychology should lead historians to broader grounds of agreement.

In the reprinted selections footnotes appearing in the original selections have in general been omitted unless they contribute to the argument or better understanding of the selection.

In this selection the eminent authority JAMES FORD
RHODES (1848–1927), a successful business man turned
historian, discusses Lincoln's "dictatorship," likening the
American chief executive to a Tudor monarch, Oliver
Cromwell, and to Louis XIV. For the ten weeks between
the surrender of Sumter and the convening of Congress
into special session, the President ruled the Republic.
Throughout the war he assumed extraordinary powers.
Rhodes begins with Lincoln's own statement, made in his
July 4, 1861, message to Congress, of the emergency
measures he took without congresssional sanction. Note the
measures and their relation to the Constitution, the
response of Congress, and Rhodes's evaluation of the
dictator. The second portion of the selection deals with
personal liberty in wartime. What were the liberties at
issue? How does Rhodes go about appraising executive
abridgment of constitutional guarantees? What is his
judgment of the extrajudicial procedure and of the
President?*

James Ford Rhodes

Lincoln's "Dictatorship"

Congress met in Washington July 4. On
the next day the President's message was
read in the Senate and the House, the representatives testifying their approval of
many parts of it by enthusiastic applause.
The President asked Congress for at least
400,000 men and $400,000,000, in order to
make "this contest a short and decisive
one." Congress gave him authority to accept the services of 500,000 volunteers and,
carrying out substantially the more detailed recommendation of the Secretary of
the Treasury, authorized a loan of
$250,000,000; it also increased the tariff
duties, provided for a direct tax of

$20,000,000, apportioned to all the States
and territories, and imposed an income-
tax, hoping from this legislation to get a
revenue of about $75,000,000 for the fiscal
year.

The President spoke in his message of
his extraordinary acts since Sumter fell.
He believed that the call for 75,000 militia
and the proclamation of the blockade were
strictly legal. The call for three-years
troops and the increase of the regular army
and navy were measures which, if not
strictly legal, he trusted then and now that
Congress would readily ratify. He had
deemed it necessary to the public safety to

*From James Ford Rhodes, *History of the United States from the Compromise of 1850* (7 vols.; New York: The
Macmillan Company, 1893–1906), vol. III, pp 437–442; vol. IV, pp. 228–235. Footnotes omitted.

authorize the commanding general to suspend the privilege of the writ of *habeas corpus,* in justification of which he made the argument of necessity, but he also reasoned that it was no violation of the Constitution. This subject from the first engaged the attention of Congress, and a joint resolution was introduced to approve and confirm these several acts. The extreme Democrats opposed this violently; but though their arguments were forcible, they had the defect of applying to a state of war considerations mainly applicable only to a condition of peace. It was more important, however, that Republicans and the Democrats who were disposed to co-operate with them in all measures for the vigorous prosecution of the war to restore the Union differed in regard to these points. There was a concord of opinion that the call for 75,000 militia and the proclamation of blockade were strictly legal, but able jurists out of Congress and lawyers and statesmen of the Senate did not agree about the suspension of the privilege of the writ of *habeas corpus.* The notion prevailed that the call for three-years volunteers and the increase of the army and the navy by proclamation was an assumption of powers by the executive which the Constitution strictly and unmistakably vested solely in Congress, and that the argument that they did not involve a violation of the organic act was strained. In the last days of the session there was tacked to the bill for the increase of the pay of the privates in the army a section ratifying the acts and proclamations of the President respecting the regular army and navy and the militia and volunteers from the States. This passed the Senate with only five negative votes, all five being from the border slave States. On a test vote in the House nineteen opposed such action.

Lincoln, in his message, spoke not only to Congress, but to the people—the "plain people," as he called them; and no one understood them better than he. He told them how he regretted the war, and made it clear that it had been forced upon him. He related, by the aid of a familiar illustration, the course of the secessionists, combated their argument, and gave, in emphatic and easily understood words, the theory on which the resistance of the government to the "rebellion" was based. He told them the meaning and the purpose of the conflict; he explained the reason of the war. "This is essentially a people's contest," he declared. "The leading object of the government for whose existence we contend" is "to afford all an unfettered start and a fair chance in the race of life." Such a government the secessionists aim to overthrow, and "the plain people understand and appreciate this." Many of the officers of the army and the navy in high station have "proved false to the hand which had pampered tl.em," but "not one common soldier or common sailor is known to have deserted his flag.... This is the patriotic instinct of plain people. They understand without an argument that the destroying the government which was made by Washington means no good to them." They have therefore rushed to its defence. "One of the greatest perplexities of the government," he said, "is to avoid receiving troops faster than it can provide for them. In a word, the people will save their government, if the government itself will do its part only indifferently well." "And having thus chosen our course, without guile and with pure purpose," he concluded, "let us renew our trust in God, and go forward without fear and with manly hearts."

No demagogue ever made a more crafty appeal, and yet nothing could be further from the appeal of a demagogue. In manners, habits of life, to a large extent in tastes, Lincoln was himself one of the "plain people"; he was separated from the mass only by his great intellectual ability. The people of the North felt him to be one of them, and since the 4th of March it had come to them, at first dimly, but steadily, though by slow degrees, that their President was a man of power, fitted to guide the nation in its crisis, and they knew that when he proclaimed anything it was the truth as he saw it. They felt that Lincoln was their true representative; that when he acted, their will was expressed. Their hearts went out to him. The relation was one of mutual confidence. He felt he had their trust. They knew their trust lay in worthy hands.

The cabinet were beginning to see that Lincoln would be the master. "Executive skill and vigor are rare qualities," privately wrote Seward. "The President is the best of us." The discussions in Congress and the action of that body show what a change of opinion had been wrought since the 4th of March concerning him in the minds of the politicians and statesmen of the nation. No ruler could hope to have his wishes more fully met by his legislature than were Lincoln's by the Congress which deliberated from July 4 to August 6. As one of its members afterwards wrote, the "session was but a giant committee of ways and means." In the Senate were 12 Democrats and 4 Unionists from the border slave States, and of these one half co-operated faithfully with the Republicans in the important measures for the vigorous prosecution of the war. The House was composed of 106 Republicans, 42 Democrats, and 28 Unionists; but on the resolution offered by McClernand, a Democrat, that the House pledge itself "to vote for any amount of money and any number of men which may be necessary to insure a speedy and effectual suppression of the rebellion," there were only 5 nays. This substantial unanimity of Congress, its members bred

in an atmosphere of liberty and having a profound respect for the law, was the more remarkable inasmuch as the acts of the President since April 15 had been the acts of a Tudor rather than those of a constitutional ruler. He had encroached on the legislature, a department of our government always jealous for the limits of its authority. "One of the most interesting features of the present state of things," wrote Schleiden to Sumner, "is the illimited power exercised by the government. Mr. Lincoln is, in that respect, the equal, if not the superior, of Louis Napoleon. The difference consists only in the fact that the President rests his authority on the unanimous consent of the people of the loyal States, the emperor his on the army." Lincoln was strong with Congress; he was stronger still with the people. The country attorney of Illinois had assumed the power of a dictator. Congress agreed that the times needed one, and the people backed their President. Yet there was method in this trust, for never had the power of dictator fallen into safer and nobler hands. . . .

More severe criticism than is due for any positive action in the House or the Senate must be meted out to the leaders of the party for their speeches in and out of the legislative halls, and to the influential Democratic newspapers in their effort to form and guide a public sentiment which should dictate the policy of the government. One fact they ignored, that peace was impossible unless the Southern Confederacy were acknowledged and a boundary line agreed upon between what then would be two distinct nations. They pretended to a belief, for which there was absolutely no foundation, that if fighting ceased and a convention of the States were called, the Union might be restored. Hence proceeded their opposition to the emancipation policy of the President as being an obstacle to the two sections coming together. But men who loved their country better than their party ought to have perceived, for it was palpable at the time, that the Southern States had not the vaguest notion of consenting on even the most favorable conditions to the Union as it was, and that the President had been brought to his decree against slavery by the logic of events. Apologists for slavery as the Democrats had been for so many years on the ground that it was a necessary evil, they could not give hearty support to emancipation, but, influenced by the consideration that slavery was morally wrong, they could with patriotism and consistency adopt the position of Henderson, the Unionist senator from Missouri, that the proclamation was a military order, and, having been made, should be executed. Without the pursuit of an impossible attainment, without a factious opposition to the acts of the President and Congress, there remained scope for a healthy opposition which would not have left the name Copperhead-Democrat a reproach for so many years; in truth, the Democrats might have deserved well of the muse of history. Indeed they did well in advocating economy and integrity in the disposition of the public money, and they might have gone further and applauded Chase in his efforts to secure the one and Stanton in his determination to have the other. Their criticisms of the Executive for suspending the privilege of the writ of *habeas corpus,* for arbitrary arrests, for the abridgment of the freedom of speech and of writing, were justly taken, and undoubtedly had an influence for the good on the legislation at this session. Had they concentrated their opposition on these points, their arguments would have carried greater force, and would have attracted men who were disturbed at the infractions of personal lib-

erty, but who were repelled by the other parts of the Democratic programme.

In consideration of our own practice, the decision of our courts, the opinions of our statesmen and jurists, and English precedents for two centuries, it may be affirmed that the right of suspending the privilege of the writ of *habeas corpus* was vested by the Constitution in Congress and not in the executive. The President, in assuming that authority and applying the suspension to States beyond the sphere of hostile operations, arrogated power which became necessary to support the policy of arbitrary arrests so diligently pursued by Seward at first and afterwards by Stanton. Such pretensions that revolt the spirit born to freedom may be oppugned by arguments drawn from the storehouse of British and American liberty. The defence made was that these things were done under the pressure of necessity. Our own precedents were set aside because our State now stood in its greatest peril since the adoption of the Constitution. Still, in England during the years of the war against the revolutionary government of France, when discontent at home and the sympathy of a band of reformers with the Democratic sentiment across the channel scared the statesmen and the bulk of the upper and middle classes, who were agitated by the terrors of the French Revolution, into a belief that the Constitution and the throne were in danger, neither the King nor the ministry claimed the right to suspend the *habeas corpus* act. It was done by Parliament, which limited in each of the acts passed the suspension to less than one year. When this time expired the ministry were obliged to bring in a new bill which was open to debate in both houses. Summing up the months covered by different measures, Parliament granted the withdrawal of the privilege for only five out of the nine years of the war. Besides, men, though arbitrarily detained, were arrested according to law. Acts were passed to suit the exigency of the time, and many of the suspects were brought to trial before a jury in the civil courts. From April to December, 1798—the period, as it appears, of the largest number of arrests—seventy or eighty persons had been apprehended but not brought to trial. At the time of the earnest discussion of such violations of personal liberty in the House of Commons in December, only a few still remained in prison; and the place of their confinement had become known as the Bastile. From May, 1799, to February, 1800, but three men had been arrested; yet it was a subject of indignant remonstrance by two lords in a session of their body that twenty-nine persons were still immured in jail without being brought to trial. In our own country during the civil war the number of arrests of political prisoners must be counted by thousands. In England lists of the prisoners had been called for and sent to both houses of Parliament. By the act of March 3, 1863, the Secretary of State and the Secretary of War were required to furnish lists of "State or political prisoners" to the judges of the United States Courts, but no lists, so far as I have been able to ascertain, were ever furnished; and in truth the relish for autocratic government had so developed that in September of this year Chase was surprised that the provisions of this act were unfamiliar to the President and to all the members of the cabinet except himself.

In both countries those opposed to the government called the state of things a "reign of terror"; in both cases the phrase was a misnomer; in neither country up to the present time have the great principles of liberty been invalidated by the exercise in its crisis of those extraordinary powers. In Great Britain the government displayed

method in its rigor. It instituted prosecutions in Scotland, where, the rule being different from that in England, the courts had "unrestricted power to visit sedition with the penalty of transportation" and cruel punishments were inflicted for insignificant offences. The special acts of Parliament were more comprehensive and severe than those of Congress, and they led in England to prosecutions which were unreasonable and unjust. In the comparison one is struck with the more careful observance of the forms of law in the older country. Most of the harshness was committed in a regular manner which was rendered easier by the subservience of Parliament to the king and the ministry, the stricter execution of the laws in the Great Britain of 1793–1802 than in the United States of 1861–65, and the greater devotion of the bench to the government. In Scotland this subordination amounted to servility: indeed one judge instructed the jury in a charge that bestowed upon him the nickname of Jeffreys. With us there were no individual cases of so extreme hardship as in Scotland. Four able and educated men were sentenced to fourteen years' transportation to Botany Bay because they had advocated parliamentary reform and universal suffrage. It falls not to me to tell a tale of suffering on board the hulks, of the lives of aspiring men crushed by the cruelty of the law, nor have I to mention a monument like the Martyrs' Memorial on Calton Hill in Edinburgh; but, on account of the wholesale violations of personal liberty by our government, it well may be that the mass of suffering in our land was even greater.

After careful consideration of our own case, I do not hesitate to condemn the arbitrary arrests and the arbitrary interference with the freedom of the press in States which were not the theatre of the war and where the courts were open. I do not omit to take into account that, bad as was Vallandigham's speech in the House, even worse was much of the writing in the Democratic newspapers; that the "Copperhead" talk on the street, in the public conveyances, and in the hotels was still more bitter and vituperative; that the virulence was on the increase, and that constant complaints of "the utterance of treasonable sentiments" were made by patriotic men to the authorities. Nevertheless I am convinced that all of this extrajudicial procedure was inexpedient, unnecessary, and wrong; that the offenders should have been prosecuted according to law, or, if their offences were not indictable, permitted to go free. "Abraham Lincoln," writes James Bryce, "wielded more authority than any single Englishman has done since Oliver Cromwell." My reading of English history and comparative study of our own have led me to the same conclusion, although it must be added that the power which Cromwell exercised far transcended that which was assumed by Lincoln, who governed with less infraction of the Constitution of his country than did the Protector of the Commonwealth. Moreover, there was in Lincoln's nature so much of kindness and mercy that he mitigated the harshness perpetrated by Seward and by Stanton. The pervasion of his individual influence, his respect for the Constitution and the law which history and tradition ascribe to him, the greatness of his character and work have prevented the generation that has grown up since the civil conflict from appreciating the enormity of the acts done under his authority by the direction of the Secretaries of State and of War. While I have not lighted upon an instance in which the President himself directed an arrest, he permitted them all; he stands responsible for the casting into prison of citizens of the United States on orders as arbitrary as the *lettres-de-cachet* of Louis XIV, instead of their apprehension, as in Great Britain in her crisis, on legal warrants.

James G. Randall

Lincoln's "Dictatorship" Reconsidered

I

Though no one expects government in
war time to be normal, yet in studying any
government it is useful to have in mind
some norm or standard in comparison with
which it may be judged. One finds such a
norm in the principle of the "rule of law"
which has been made familiar to English
and American readers through Professor
Dicey's *Law of the Constitution*. It will be
worth while to recall what this principle
involves in order to have it in view while
commenting on governmental practice under Lincoln's presidency. In England, as
Professor Dicey shows, the "rule of law"
means that every man's legal rights or lia-
bilities are almost invariably determined
by the ordinary courts; that executive officers have a more limited discretion and
less arbitrary power than in other European countries; and that no man is above
the law, but all are amenable to the juris-
diction of the ordinary tribunals, officers
being personally liable for wrongs done,
even though in an official capacity. He
adds that personal rights in England do
not derive from a constitution but inherently exist.

American political philosophy is in accord with this principle. Our ideal, it has
been said, is a "government of laws, not of
men." Law is above government: government is under law. Martial law, while
sometimes used in this country, is viewed
with distrust and is regarded as abnormal.
We think of it as the setting aside of law,
not as its fulfillment. The military power

*From James G. Randall, *Constitutional Problems Under Lincoln*, Revised edition (Urbana, Ill.: University
of Illinois Press, 1951), pp. 511–522. Footnotes omitted.

we believe to be subordinate to the civil; and even amid serious disturbances we have preferred to rely upon civil procedure. There is in this country a deplorable disregard for law as it restrains individuals; but this is entirely consistent with that other disposition to subject our rulers to legal restraints. Our respect for the Supreme Court is typical of our attitude in this matter.

Nor is it conformable to American political philosophy to hold that during war legal restraints are to be ignored. The maxim "necessity knows no law" appears to the American legal genius as a half-truth rather than a fundamental or central principle. Too often the maxim is a mere excuse. Unrestrained military power even in war is repugnant to the American mind. International law (which includes the "laws of civilized warfare"), treaty obligations, and at least a proximate preservation of civil rights (not ignoring those of an enemy population under military occupation) are factors which should restrain any warring government. The view that prevails in America is that even amid arms the laws hold; and one of the great doctrines of the Supreme Court, as announced in the Milligan case, is that the Constitution is not suspended during war.

This conception of a reign of law is, of course, but an ideal. We believe that the settled, permanent will of the whole community, as expressed in fundamental law, is a great stabilizing force; and in the ordering of our political life we believe that every effort should be made to give superior force to our mature, sober judgment as against the designs of our rulers.

The ideal is never realized, but such is the manner of ideals. Though in a sense we always live under a government of men, yet the rule of law as a standard has its definite value none the less.

II

When the Government under Lincoln is set over against this standard, its irregular and extra-legal characteristics become conspicuous. It is indeed a striking fact that Lincoln, who stands forth in popular conception as a great democrat, the exponent of liberty and of government by the people, was driven by circumstances to the use of more arbitrary power than perhaps any other President has seized. Probably no President has carried the power of proclamation and executive order (independently of Congress) so far as did Lincoln. It would not be easy to state what Lincoln conceived to be the limit of his powers. He carried his executive authority to the extent of freeing the slaves by proclamation, setting up a whole scheme of state-making for the purpose of reconstruction, suspending the *habeas corpus* privilege, proclaiming martial law, enlarging the army and navy beyond the limits fixed by existing law, and spending public money without congressional appropriation. Some of his important measures were taken under the consciousness that they belonged within the domain of Congress. The national legislature was merely permitted to ratify these measures, or else to adopt the futile alternative of refusing consent to an accomplished fact. We have seen how the first national use of conscription, in connection with the Militia Act of 1862,[1] was an instance of presidential legislation. We have also noted the exercise of judicial functions by Lincoln or those acting under his authority, in regions under martial law, in Southern territory under Union occupation, in the application of military justice, in the performance of quasi-judicial func-

---

[1] The act referred to "enrolling" and "calling forth" the militia, but it did not specifically provide for a draft. Nevertheless, under it, Lincoln ordered the drafting of Federal troops.—Ed.

tions by executive departments, and in the creation of "special war courts" such as the "provisional court of Louisiana." It thus appears that the President, while greatly enlarging his executive powers, seized also legislative and judicial functions as well.

Lincoln's view of the war power is significant. He believed that rights of war were vested in the President, and that as President he had extraordinary legal resources which Congress lacked. For example, he promulgated the "laws of war" to regulate the conduct of the armies; and in vetoing the Wade-Davis bill of 1864 he questioned the constitutional competency of Congress to abolish slavery in the States at a time when his own edict of emancipation had been in force for eighteen months. Lincoln tended to the view that in war the Constitution restrains Congress more than it restrains the President. Yet the view of the Supreme Court was that Congress may exercise belligerent powers and that in the use of these powers over the enemy the restraints of the Constitution do not apply. Lincoln's view, under pressure of severe circumstance, led naturally to that course which has been referred to as his "dictatorship"; and, as illustrated in the *Prize Cases,* it produced uncertainty as to the legality of the war. Though the validity of Lincoln's acts was sustained by a majority of the court—which could hardly have decided otherwise on so vital a political question—yet four dissenting judges held that the President's action alone was not sufficient to institute a legal state of war. Lincoln's plea in defense, to the effect that his acts within the legislative domain could be legalized by congressional ratification, could hardly be accepted as consistent with the constitutional separation of powers; and this whole phase of the President's conduct illustrates not so much a permanently acceptable principle, but rather Lincoln's ability to retain popular confidence while doing irregular things. It should be added that Lincoln excelled in human reasonableness, and that his character included not only a readiness to act in an emergency, but also a high regard for the rule of law.

III

In all this extension of governmental power there was a noticeable lack of legal precision. A tendency toward irregularity may be observed as a characteristic of the period, in military and civil administration, in legislation, and in legal interpretation. Congress did its work loosely and various of its laws were never carried out; while others produced bewilderment in the officers who sought to apply them. The Southern States were taxed as if part of the United States; yet the property out of which such tax must be paid was declared confiscable as belonging to enemies. The Unionist government of Virginia was considered competent to authorize the disruption of the State; but later this same government (removed from Wheeling to Alexandria) was denied representation in Congress and rejected as the instrument of reconstruction. Eight States of the former Confederacy, after assisting in ratifying the anti-slavery amendment of the Constitution, were treated as outside the Union. Legal interpretation in the 'sixties often smacked of sophistry—so much so that to many men an open confession of unconstitutionality appeared preferable to the labored reasoning that was all too common. Much of the legal inconsistency arose from confusion as to what the war was, whether it was extramural or within the family. Was the Government facing something like a magnified Whiskey Insurrection, or was it dealing with war in the international sense? Confronted with this dilemma, the Supreme Court adopted the convenient and practical solution of accepting both alternatives.

The conflict was defined as both a public war and a rebellion, with the result that in Southern territory the United States claimed both belligerent and municipal powers. Many bootless and mystifying discussions resulted from this acceptance of two inconsistent viewpoints.

Yet there was nothing more natural than that these two opposite theories of the war should both be adopted. As to the insurrectionary theory, its adoption resulted from the Government's unwillingness to accept disunion as justified and to give up Federal sovereignty in the South; while the recognition of the struggle as a public war arose from the practical necessity of dealing with a nation in arms as a regular belligerent. The existence side by side of two opposing legal principles is understandable if we remember that the insurrectionary theory was not in fact applied as against Southern leaders and their adherents. They were not held personally liable as insurrectionists as were the leaders of the Whiskey Insurrection; instead, the Confederacy was in practice treated as a government with belligerent powers.

I V

If we were to ask how far our usual constitutional checks operated during the Civil War to prevent an extreme use of power, we would find that neither Congress nor the Supreme Court exercised any very effective restraint upon the President. Congress specifically approved the President's course between April and July, 1861;[2] and, as to the *habeas corpus* question, after two years' delay, Congress passed an ambiguous law which was at the same time interpreted as approving and disap-

proving the doctrine that the President has the suspending power. The net effect, however, was to support the President; and immunity from prosecution was granted to officers who committed wrongs during the suspension. It is true that the Habeas Corpus Act of 1863 directed the release of prisoners unless indicted in the courts. This was equivalent to saying that the President's suspension of the privilege, which was authorized by this act, was to be effective in any judicial district only until a grand jury should meet. On paper this law radically altered the whole system regarding political prisoners, making arbitrary imprisonment illegal after grand juries had examined the prisoners' cases. The significant fact, however, is that the law was ineffective. It did not, in fact, put an end to extra-legal imprisonments; nor did it succeed in shifting the control of punishments from executive and military hands to judicial hands.

As to the courts, a careful study will show that they did not function in such a way as to control the emergency. In dealing with disloyal practices the courts played a passive rather than an active rôle. They dealt in a hesitating way with cases that were brought to them; but the President, through the Attorney General and the district attorneys, controlled the prosecutions, and where it appeared that treason indictments were being pushed toward conviction, the administration at Washington showed actual embarrassment at the Government's success. Its way of dealing with dangerous citizens was not by prosecution in the courts, but by arbitrary imprisonment, followed by arbitrary release. The terrors of the old treason law proving unsuitable to the emergency, its penalty was softened; but even the softened penalty was not enforced. There is a striking contrast between the great number of arbitrary arrests and the almost negligible

---

[2] During these months Lincoln conducted the war single-handed, without congressional authorization.—Ed.

amount of completed judicial action for treason, conspiracy, and obstructing the draft. It was widely argued that the courts could not deal with the emergency, and that this inability justified an extraordinary extension of military power.

The Supreme Court of the United States did not, during the war, exert any serious check upon either Congress or the President. In the *Prize Cases* the court approved Lincoln's acts in the early months of the war. Such an extreme measure as confiscation was upheld by the court, though its validity, both in the international and the constitutional sense, was seriously questioned. It was not the Supreme Court, but Chief Justice Taney, hearing the Merryman petition in chambers, who denounced the President's suspension of the *habeas corpus* privilege. After the war, it is true, the court, in the Milligan case, declared a military régime illegal in regions remote from the theater of war; but while the war was in progress the court had declined to interfere with the action of a military commission in a similar case, that of Vallandigham. On the whole it appears that, while extreme measures were being taken, neither Congress nor the courts exerted any effective restraint. Instead of the "rule of law" prevailing, as Dicey defined it, men were imprisoned outside the law and independently of the courts; and governmental officers were given a privileged place above the law and made immune from penalties for wrongs committed.

V

This is one side of the picture. There is, however, another side; and we must note certain factors which at least partly redeemed the situation. The greatest factor, perhaps, was the legal-mindedness of the American people; and a very great factor was Lincoln himself. His humane sympathy, his humor, his lawyerlike caution, his common sense, his fairness toward opponents, his dislike of arbitrary rule, his willingness to take the people into his confidence and to set forth patiently the reasons for unusual measures—all these elements of his character operated to modify and soften the acts of overzealous subordinates and to lessen the effect of harsh measures upon individuals. He was criticized for leniency as often as for severity. Though there were arbitrary arrests under Lincoln, there was no thoroughgoing arbitrary government. The Government smarted under great abuse without passing either an Espionage Act or a Sedition Law. Freedom of speech was preserved to the point of permitting the most disloyal utterances. While a book could be written on the suppression of certain newspapers, the military control of the telegraph, the seizure of particular editions, the withholding of papers from the mails, and the arrest of editors, yet in a broad view of the whole situation such measures appear so far from typical that they sink into comparative insignificance. There was no real censorship, and in the broad sense the press was unhampered though engaging in activities distinctly harmful to the Government. As to Lincoln's attitude in this matter, it should be remembered that in general he advised non-interference with the press, and that he applied this policy prominently in the case of the Chicago *Times*.

To suppose that Lincoln's suspension of the *habeas corpus* privilege set aside all law would be erroneous. The suspension was indeed a serious matter; but men were simply arrested on suspicion, detained for a while, and then released. The whole effect of their treatment was milder than if they had been punished through the ordinary processes of justice. As to the military trial of civilians, it should be noticed that the typical use of the military commission was legitimate; for these commissions were ommonly used to try citizens in military reas for military crimes. Where citizens in roximity to the Union army were engaged in sniping or bushwhacking, in ridge burning or the destruction of ailroad or telegraph lines, they were tried, s they should have been, by military commission; and this has occasioned little comment, though there were hundreds of ases. The prominence of the cases of Valndigham and Milligan should not obcure the larger fact that these cases were xceptional: in other words, the military ial of citizens for non-military offenses in eaceful areas was far from typical. It was us a rare use of the military commission at was declared illegal in the Milligan ase.

Legally, the Civil War stands out as an ccentric period, a time when constitution-l restraints did not fully operate and hen the "rule of law" largely broke own. It was a period when opposite and nflicting situations coexisted, when speous arguments and legal fictions were put rth to excuse extraordinary measures. It as a period during which the line was lurred between executive, legislative, and dicial functions; between State and Fedal powers; and between military and civprocedures. International law as well as nstitutional interpretation was stretched. he powers grasped by Lincoln caused m to be denounced as a "dictator." Yet civil liberties were not annihilated and no thoroughgoing dictatorship was established. There was nothing like a Napoleonic *coup d'état*. No undue advantage was taken of the emergency to force arbitrary rule upon the country or to promote personal ends. A comparison with European examples shows that Lincoln's government lacked many of the earmarks of dictatorial rule. His administration did not, as in some dictatorships, employ criminal violence to destroy its opponents and perpetuate its power. It is significant that Lincoln half expected to be defeated in 1864. The people were free to defeat him, if they chose, at the polls. The Constitution, while stretched, was not subverted. The measures taken were recognized by the people as exceptional; and they were no more exceptional than the emergency for which they were used. Looking beyond the period called "reconstruction," the net effect, as Lincoln had said, was not to give the nation a taste for extreme rule any more than a patient, because of the use of emetics during illness, acquired a taste for them in normal life. In a legal study of the war the two most significant facts are perhaps these: the wide extent of the war powers; and, in contrast to that, the manner in which the men in authority were nevertheless controlled by the American people's sense of constitutional government.

A different point of view is presented in a painstaking study of Lincoln and the patronage by HARRY J. CARMAN (1884–1964), who taught history at Columb University and served as dean of the college, and REINHARD H. LUTHIN (1905–1962), a specialist on Lincoln who taught at Columbia and became a free-lan writer of history. They consider the President neither as dictator, a spoilsmonger, a prey of Radicals or state governors, nor as beset by Copperheads, but as a practic politician resourcefully employing the appointment pow They appraise how he used the spoils system, its effects upon Republican factionalism, upon party leadership, a upon national unity. Besides pondering these problems, the reader may ask himself: Is there a contradiction between partisanship and statesmanship, or can the two successfully combined?*

Harry J. Carman and Reinhard H. Luthin

Lincoln Distributes the Spoils

Abraham Lincoln came to the presidency in the halcyon days of the spoils system and when pressure for a "clean sweep" on the part of the victor had never been more insistent. As far as is known, Lincoln prior to 1861 did not oppose this practice and, although he made no ante-nomination promises, once elected he operated along customary lines. Indeed, the change in party control from Democrats to Republicans was the occasion for the most sweeping removal of federal officeholders up to that time in American history. Of the 1,520 presidential officeholders no less than 1,195 were removed as a result of the Republican victory of 1860— an almost complete sweep if allowance is made for the vacancies in the South occa-

sioned by the Secession. Undoubtedly few in office by President Buchanan's a pointment continued to hold their jobs u der Lincoln. They were primarily the whose efficiency raised them above par such as William Hunter, retained in t Department of State; John J. Cisco, Su Treasurer at New York; James W. Tayl Treasury Agent in Canada; and Elis Whittlesey, Comptroller of the Treasury.

Though changes in office under Linc were considerably more numerous tha usual, they varied from department to d partment according to the disposition those who administered the patronage. S ward, for example, did not make wholesa changes in the State Department; on t other hand, the master-spoilsman, Car

*From Harry J. Carman and Reinhard H. Luthin, *Lincoln and the Patronage* (New York: Columbia Univers Press, 1943), pp. 331–336. Footnotes omitted.

on, early intimated to War Department
rks "that most of them would be ex-
cted to retire, for others who had not
joyed the flesh-pots."

How many sinecure appointments ex-
ed during Lincoln's administration we
not know. Probably they could be
nd in every department. Under date of
ne 7, 1862, we find A. B. Mullett writing
ase as follows:

ave been assigned to a regular desk in your
reau where I am engaged in keeping a book
ented by Mr. Shannon, the chief merit of
ich is its utter uselessness for any other purse than as an excuse for a Clerk. . . . The
sition is . . . one of the sinecures so abundant
the Department. And I am sure you should
astonished if you knew how little work is
ne by some, and how much useless work by
er Clerks in the Department, as well as the
mbersome . . . methods that are in use gen-
lly.

The preceding pages of this book leave
tle doubt that Lincoln distributed the
tronage probably as wisely as any hu-
an could under the circumstances. No
esident of the United States, perhaps,
s ever confronted by a more difficult situ-
ion. Not only did he face the task of
eping together a party composed of di-
rse elements, each thinking that its labors
d been decisive in electing him to the
tion's highest office, but he had to hold
e allegiance of all those outside his party
o loyally supported the Union. Further-
ore, his renomination and re-election for
econd term could not be ignored.

Factionalism and wirepulling within his
n party were especially vexatious. Nota-
y was this true in New York, Illinois,
nnsylvania, and Indiana, where in 1861
e factions grouped themselves into a
ward–Weed–David Davis–Cameron–
aleb B. Smith alliance and a Barney–
illiam Cullen Bryant–Judd–McClure–
olfax entente. In the formation of his

Cabinet Lincoln was subjected to great
pressure by both of these powerful groups.
The former wanted Cameron in the Cabinet and Chase excluded; the latter
wanted Chase appointed and Cameron
excluded. To preserve harmony, Lincoln
reluctantly took Cameron but refused to
exclude Chase. This action was in keeping
with his constant effort to balance or to ad-
just properly the claims of the various factions that made up the party.

For his initial Cabinet Lincoln brought
together a heterogeneous group. In se-
lecting his inner council he was governed
by a variety of motives: recognition of rivals
within the party, political antecedents,
pivotal states, geographical regions, and
pledges made by his managers. Yet his
Cabinet was far from being a harmonious
unit. Each member had been more or less
of a political leader in his home state. Four
of them—Seward, Chase, Cameron, and
Bates—were defeated candidates for the
elevated chair held by Lincoln. Moreover,
both Whig and non-Whig or radical points
of view were represented. It is a rather remarkable tribute to Lincoln that, with the
exception of Chase, he increasingly gained
the confidence and respect of his Cabinet
members. Not immediately, but ultimately, they acquired the habit of turning to
him, like quarreling children to their
mother, to settle the questions that temporarily divided them.

In making appointments Lincoln followed practices that were in keeping with
American political tradition. He consulted
members of the upper house in making
nominations for or from their states. Minor
offices were generally given to those nominated by members of the House of Representatives. Lincoln also listened to governors, especially of important or pivotal
states. Heads of departments and certain
powerful nonofficeholding individuals,
such as Thurlow Weed, were influential

with Lincoln. Though he patiently gave ear to all requests irrespective of source, the President did not submit to dictation, unless the removal of Montgomery Blair from the Postmaster Generalship be so interpreted. Although Mrs. Lincoln on more than one occasion tried to take a hand in politics, the evidence is not sufficient that her efforts were a controlling factor in influencing Lincoln's action. The attempt of Chase, as we have observed, to have his way in the matter of appointments made for unpleasantness and ultimately was a major reason for Lincoln's acceptance of Chase's resignation as Secretary of the Treasury.

Military appointments were made in much the same way as those in the civil service. In naming men to army posts, however, Lincoln found it desirable to call on Democrats. But in making civil appointments, the President almost invariably selected Republicans. Moreover, it would seem that Lincoln, except in a few cases, made no very searching effort to ascertain whether the persons appointed were those best fitted by talent and experience for the job. In other words, he followed the time-honored rule of political expediency. To friends—particularly those of long standing—he was inclined to show favoritism. Nepotism was not entirely absent.

In the slave regions Lincoln encountered a difficult situation. In the "loyal" border states of Missouri and Maryland patronage problems were acute, aggravated by the split of the Republican-Union party into conservatives and radicals. In distributing the federal jobs Lincoln endeavored, as we have noted, to appease both factions in these states, but not always did his maxim "Justice to All" prove practicable. In Missouri he found it more expedient to give the edge to the conservative Blair interests, but in Maryland he found

it equally expedient to favor the Blair avowed enemies, the radical followers Henry Winter Davis.

That Lincoln utilized the patronage f purely political ends is evident in the num ber of federal officeholders who partic pated in the movement to secure his r nomination for the presidency in 186 Professor James G. Randall succinct summarizes the story:

Lincoln's managers had been active. They h the advantage of controlling the regular R publican (Union) party, in which they held t managerial positions; they had the patronag including provost marshals, postmasters, a Federal employees the country over; they h the disposal of contracts; and they work through state conventions in which delegates the national convention were instructed Lincoln. When the Republican Conventi met at Baltimore on June 7 the effectiveness organization and regularity in American polit was impressively demonstrated.

During the campaign for re-election the summer and early fall of 1864, Linco found it necessary to make certain remo als for the sake of victory in Novembe We need only remind the reader that placate the radicals and to foster the mov ment for Frémont's withdrawal from t presidential race, Lincoln requested t conservative Montgomery Blair to give the Postmaster Generalship. To concilia the conservatives and bring greater ha mony to his official family and to t party, he accepted Chase's proffered resi nation from the Treasuryship.

Following Lincoln's re-election in N vember, 1864, new troubles broke o within the party. In the creation of t complex, intricate, and bitter struggle b tween conservatives and radicals, rivalry f public office seemed at times to have be almost as potent a source of discord b tween the two main factions as difference opinion over the Reconstruction policy be adopted toward the crumbling states of the Confederacy.

The criticism that Lincoln gave too much time to patronage, especially during the early weeks of his administration— time that could have been utilized to effect a settlement with the South before the opening of hostilities—is perhaps not entirely justified. Under the circumstances it is difficult to see how the matter could have been handled otherwise. To have entrusted it to an underling less astute politically than was Lincoln would have been unwise. The defense of Lincoln on this point by his Secretary of the Navy, Gideon Welles, is apt:

In striving to reconcile and bring into united action opposing views he [Lincoln] was accused of wasting his time in a great emergency on mere party appointments. Under the pressure and influence that were brought to bear upon him some things were doubtless done, which, under other circumstances and left to himself he would have ordered differently. Extensive removals and appointments were not only expected, but absolutely necessary, yet never under any administration were greater care and deliberation required. A host of ravenous partisans from Maine to California . . . who had participated in the election of Mr. Lincoln filled Washington and besieged the White House and Departments, demanding for themselves or their friends the local appointments, regardless of the patriotism or real merits of the incumbents. This crowd of active friends with their importunities at such a crisis was of course extremely embarrassing to the new administration, which commenced its labors with a demoralized government and crumbling Union

that needed the vigilant attention of the wisest and most considerate statesmanship.

Had Lincoln led a united party he might have utilized his time and effort somewhat differently. His wise use of the patronage in holding the party together was a necessary antecedent to the formulation of any statesmanlike policy concerning the nation. Many Lincoln admirers find it distasteful—perhaps unbelievable—to recognize in their hero the shrewd practical politician that he was. But to witness how, as a politician, he utilized the patronage in holding together diverse conflicting factions in common purposes—the preservation of the Union, the success of his administration, and the rewarding of the party faithful—is only to enhance the greatness of Lincoln. Essentially a practical man, reared in the realism of the frontier and educated in the old school of Whig politics, Lincoln recognized the necessity of patronage as a weapon in party leadership under the American system. In being a competent politician, he became a statesman. Had he not displayed his ability as a politician with such signal success, it is doubtful whether he would be regarded today as a statesman. Had he not wielded the patronage so skillfully—something that his predecessor James Buchanan and his successor Andrew Johnson did not do—probably his administration would not have been as successful. Certainly his task of holding the Union together would have been more difficult.

Another view of Lincoln, as the practical politician, is presented by WILLIAM B. HESSELTINE (1902–1963), a widely influential professor of history at the University of Wisconsin. Lincoln was confronted, he states, by both the problem of factions in his party and the challenge of heading a national party that in 1860 was in reality a confederation of state organizations. Hesseltine's emphasis may be compared with that of Carman and Luthin. The governors elected Lincoln, Hesseltine asserts, and the President had the twofold political task of subordinating the politicians in the states and combating factionalism in the national forum. How well he succeeded, the reader must judge, keeping in mind the claim in the preceding selection.*

William B. Hesseltine

Lincoln Builds a National Party

The people, declared the twenty-eight-year-old legislator, were not suffering great injuries. "No Sir, it is the *politician* who is the first to sound the alarm. ... It is he, who, by these unholy means, is endeavoring to blow up a storm that he may ride upon and direct. ... This movement is exclusively the work of politicians; a set of men who have interests aside from the interests of the people, and who, to say the most of them, are, taken as a mass, at least one long step removed from honest men."

For the remaining half of his life, Abraham Lincoln clung to his opinion of politicians. Although he added the ruefully facetious remark, "I say this with the greater freedom because, being a politician myself, none can regard it as personal," he mainly reserved the term for his opponents, and

especially for Democrats. "If the politicians and leaders of parties were as true as the people, there would be little fear," he told a crowd in Lawrenceburg, Indiana on his fifty-second birthday, and three days later, in Pittsburgh, he explained in words reminiscent of his speech in the Illinois legislature "... *there is no crisis,* except such a one as may be gotten up at any time by designing politicians." "You are quite a female politician," he told Jesse Frémont when she irritated him by explaining the effect her husband's emancipation order would have on British sentiment. "May I inquire how long it took you and the New York politicians to concoct that paper?" he asked a group of Tennesseans who protested against Andrew Johnson's arrangements for the election of 1864.

*William B. Hesseltine, "Abraham Lincoln and the Politicians," *Civil War History,* VI (March, 1960), pp. 43–55. Footnotes omitted.

Yet, however low his opinion of politicians, Abraham Lincoln took an active interest in the minutiae of politics. Formally he could advise a Young Man's Lyceum to let "reverence for the laws . . . become the political religion of the nation," while from the elevated post of congressman he could instruct young Billy Herndon on forming a "Rough and Ready Club." "Take in everybody you can get . . . gather up all the shrewd wild boys about town. . . . Let everyone play the part he can play best— some speak, some sing, and all hollow." He added example to precept. He attended meetings, and, with more talent for speaking than for singing, he spoke on every occasion. He carefully surveyed the prospects of the Whigs in each electoral campaign, and once stood for election to the legislature only to resign upon winning. "I only allowed myself to be elected," he explained, "because it was thought my doing so would help [Richard] Yates." He understood the necessity for preparing careful lists of voters and organizing them—and even for "working so quiet that the adversary shall not be notified." As for money, its use, "in the main," was wrong—"but for certain objects, in a political contest, the use of some, is both right and indispensable." So saying, he promised one hundred dollars to a prospective delegate to the Chicago Wigwam. With so intimate a knowledge of the precepts and practice of politics, Lincoln found it easy, as president-elect, to deal with such experienced political engineers as Thurlow Weed and Simon Cameron.

He was fully, even keenly, aware of the role of patronage in building and maintaining a political party. When rumor reached Illinois in 1849 that Zachary Taylor was about to appoint Justin Butterfield as Commissioner of the General Land Office, Lincoln raised a hue and cry and wrote vigorously to leading Whigs to bring pressure on the president. Butterfield's appointment, he assured them, would be an "egregious political blunder." It would "dissatisfy, rather than gratify," the Whigs of Illinois. Butterfield was a "drone" who had never spent a dollar or lifted a finger in the fight." "Shall this thing be?" he cried in anguish. "Our Whigs will throw down their arms and fight no more."

Although he opposed Butterfield, Lincoln deplored factional rivalries for patronage crumbs. Struggles for political succession weakened parties. He made a virtue of his own inability to succeed himself in Congress, and used it to emphasize his "live and let live" policy. He refused to compete for the General Land Office post he would have liked, and tried to patch up a quarrel between two rival candidates for the place. Withal, he was convinced, he told the Secretary of the Treasury, that national patronage should be dispensed through the advice of congressmen, and that President Taylor should not shirk his duty of leadership. "He must occasionally say, or seem to say, 'by the Eternal, I take the responsibility.' " Those were the lessons Jackson had taught—"and we dare not disregard the lessons of experience."

With such ideas, and with the lessons of Jackson and Taylor both confirming them, Lincoln tackled the problems of the patronage in his own administration. It was, he quickly discovered, an unending task and he moaned frequently, even sometimes with humor, at the importunities of the office seekers. When he got the varioloid smallpox he wryly remarked that now he had something he could give everyone. No sooner was he nominated than well-wishers began to advise him to avoid factionalism in the party. William Cullen Bryant warned him against politicians interested only in their own advancement, and in words reminiscent of those that Nicholas Biddle gave to William Henry Harrison, proposed that Lincoln should give no pledges, make no speeches, write no letters. Lincoln assured him that he knew the danger and meant to avoid it. "Fairness to all" became his motto, and during the campaign he added as instruction to his workers "but commit me to nothing." In August, 1860, he could assure Cassius M. Clay, who was so generally excluded from inner circles that he had come to suspect all gatherings as conspiracies, that "the cliques have not yet commenced upon me."

After November he could no longer make such a statement. The cliques come down upon him; office-seekers and their supporters swarmed upon Springfield, followed him to Washington, and settled in his waiting room for the four years that he was in the White House. "Fairness to all" continued his watchword, and factionalism continued to distress him. "There is not a more foolish way of conducting a political rivalry," he sighed in 1864 when Kansas' Senator James H. Lane and Governor Thomas Carney were squabbling, "than these fierce and bitter struggles over the patronage." His early efforts to avoid the cliques won even the approval of the Democratic New York *World.* "He has convinced us that the warm interest in his success, felt by all good men, is not thrown away upon a hard, hackneyed, truckling politician."

Not all Democrats were so generous. In fact, the general tendency of the Democratic press was to apply the touchstone of partisanship to each successive act of the president, and to see him constantly bending before political pressures. Samuel Medary's *Crisis* in Columbus, Ohio, was widely influential among Democratic journals, and often set the tone of the opposition press. To Medary, Lincoln was the "mere instrument of designing cabals around him . . . influenced to the worst of acts and the most diabolical feats of folly."

He was a "mere child" led by William H. Seward and Salmon P. Chase. His first annual message had a "partisan tone," he was "neither honest, capable, nor loyal," and was completely in the hands of "abolition vipers" led by Horace Greeley. The Union Leagues, "a more desperate and bloody set of scamps than their cousins the Know Nothings," controlled him: "They dictate terms to Mr. Lincoln as though he were a mere piece of wax. Perhaps he is." He was in all things a "miserable tool"— although even Medary admitted that it would be a national calamity if Lincoln died and Hannibal Hamlin became president. In fact, the Ohio editor was so enamoured with the idea that Lincoln was a vacillating tool that he thought "if the Democrats should get control of the next Congress, Mr. Lincoln will not be the worst man they might find in the Presidential Chair. With better surroundings, we believe Mr. Lincoln would improve vastly."

It took the New York *World* a little while to adopt Medary's viewpoint. In January, 1862, it hailed Edwin M. Stanton's appointment as Secretary of War as evidence that Lincoln was "the servant of no clique, the pliant tool of no party, the self-deceived victim of no blinding fanaticism." The "practiced politicians" of his cabinet had gained no undue ascendency over him. He was, in fact, a "cool, wise, large-minded statesman." But then came September, 1862, with its Emancipation Proclamation, and the *World* saw the light. Lincoln had "been coerced by the insanity of the radicals, by the denunciation of their presses, by the threats of their governors." The proclamation was "not the measure of a statesman, but of a politician" with his eye on the approaching elections in New York. Thereafter, the *World* called steady attention to Lincoln's partisan acts. When he called for 300,000 men, it was a "satire of statesmanship." When he removed General George B. McClellan, he had "yielded once more to their [Radical's] insensate demands." When a cabinet crisis arose, Lincoln lacked "the nerve" to deal with it—"he quailed before the enemity of the excluded faction." Moreover, Lincoln's handling of the army was political, his letter to a Niagara Conference was a scheme to entrap Republicans who were deserting to John C. Frémont. But the *World's* analysis differed in the end from that of the *Crisis*. Instead of seeing with Medary that Lincoln had surrendered to faction, the New York paper saw him engaged in "dextrous trimming" between factions— giving the offices to one and adopting the principles of the other, and frustrating himself in the process. Lincoln substituted cunning for statesmanship.

In frequent instances, the Democratic spokesmen were guessing shrewdly. Many of Lincoln's acts were politically inspired, and sometimes he yielded to pressure. But the opposition, bemused by the factional conflict between moderate and radical Republicans, failed to perceive that Lincoln was using the patronage to build the Republicans into a national party with himself at its head. Lincoln kept control of the patronage, subjecting himself to the ordeal of listening to office-seekers, and doling out the appointments. Years before, he had declared that Taylor should take, or seem to take, the responsibility. Admiringly the New York *World*, before it joined the opposition, recounted that "once he puts down his foot, he puts it down firmly." He was a "self-poised and self-dependent statesman." Rare it was that he felt himself defeated by the conflicting pressures. Once he threw the problem of a Honolulu commissioner into Seward's lap: "In self-defense," he explained, "I am disposed to say 'Make a selection and send it to me!' " But such occasions were few. And even when

he did not personally take the responsibility, he set the policy. The policy was national. He consulted congressmen on appointments in their districts—even on commissions in the army. When Tyler was president, Lincoln insisted that congressmen be consulted. Now he consulted them. "So far as I understand, it is unprecedented [to] send an officer into a State against the wishes of the members of Congress and of the same party." He referred office seekers to the departments. He agreed with William P. Fessenden that Treasury appointments should have the secretary's advice and consent. But these were national officers. Lincoln made no gesture toward the local politicians or the political leaders of the states. The patronage was national, and he used it, not primarily to balance factions but to build a national party.

Lincoln's primary task as a politician was to create a national Republican Party and to mold it into a serviceable tool for the national welfare. The party which nominated him and put him into the White House was an unorganized conglomeration of opposition groups. Some of them had been loco-focos, Barnburners, and then Free Soilers in previous political incarnations. Some were anti-Nebraska Democrats, some were the battered and shattered remnants of the old Whig Party. There were in the undisciplined ranks which marched under the Republican banner, middlewestern farmers who wanted a Homestead law, Pennsylvania iron-mongers hungering for a protective tariff, newly-arrived immigrants and old Know Nothings who wanted nothing to do with each other. The party stood, in common with Breckinridge Democrats, for a Pacific Railroad and for States Rights. It was more certain on what it stood against: It was opposed to Stephen A. Douglas, James Buchanan, the Devil, and the Democrats.

Lincoln had played a minor part in preserving the confusion. In 1848 he had thought it absurd to make a platform for a national party. It was "the true philosophy of government," he said, "that congress should represent all opinions and principles, and when the wisdom of all had been compared and united" the will of the people should prevail. As the election of 1860 drew near, Lincoln advised caution on Republicans. They should not insert into state platforms items which, however popular they might be in a particular locality, would do harm to Republicans elsewhere. He pointed to the anti-foreign sentiment in Massachusetts, the enforcement of the Fugitive Slave Law in New Hampshire and its repeal in Ohio, and squatter sovereignty in Kansas. "In these things there is explosive enough to blow up half a dozen national conventions, if it gets into them." He was not "wedded" to the party platform system, and preferred to have men chosen to office on "their records and antecedents." There was but one item upon which all Republicans were agreed—opposition to the extension of slavery to the territories—and Lincoln succeeded in keeping it to the fore. Yet when he was elected—on a platform which was like a pair of suspenders, long enough for any man and short enough for any boy— Lincoln frequently asserted that the platform bound him to accept its terms and adhere to its provisions.

The mandate of the Republican Party was far from clear, and even had Lincoln attempted to conform to its vague provisions, it would have furnished no practical guide to the political situation which confronted him. There was, in fact, no national Republican Party. There were state parties—and it had been state considerations at Chicago that led the delegates to pass over the party's outstanding man and select Lincoln. Andrew Curtin feared he could not be elected governor of Pennsylvania if Seward were the nominee. Henry S. Lane thought Indiana would vote against him. Richard Yates professed to believe he could not become governor of Illinois on a ticket headed by Seward. Candidate John Andrew of Massachusetts came to Chicago to work against Seward. State, not national consideration nominated Lincoln; and it was state parties that elected him. Twenty-two of the 33 states had an organized Republican Party, and a handful were safely Republican with Republican governors and recently successful organizations full of enthusiasm. In eleven crucial states, three in New England and the others stretching westward to the Mississippi, the Republicans had vigorous gubernatorial candidates. In them the national campaign turned on the state elections. Each went Republican, and in each state, except Massachusetts and Illinois, the governor ran ahead of Lincoln. The Republican Party in the states had elected a president for the nation. If Lincoln were to weld a national party, he must first wrest control of its segments from the governors.

Since the governors had elected Lincoln, they had no hesitancy in instructing him on his program. Sewardites and moderates among the politicians counseled moderation and conciliation in the secession crisis. Tentatively, Lincoln experimented with the idea of bringing Southerners, Constitutional Unionists who had supported John Bell and Edward Everett, into his official family. William Cullen Bryant advised it, and Lincoln hoped to bring John A. Gilmer into the cabinet. But the president-elect forsaw the futility of such efforts to mend the sectional breech with patronage plaster. "We could not safely take more than one such man . . . the danger being to lose the confidence of our own friends." His friends, indeed, or a vociferous section of them, favored no conciliation with the

South. Old Barnburners assembled in New York to demand that the abolitionist Salmon P. Chase go into the cabinet. In Indiana the new governor called for an abolitionist crusade. Early in January when newly elected governors, the real or titular heads of the Republican parties, assumed office, they called for war. John Andrew struck a dramatic note in Massachusetts and found echoing response from Austin Blair in Michigan. Richard Yates instructed his constituent who was going to the White House to show firmness and wisdom and to use the military power to defend the constitution. By the time of his inauguration, Lincoln had heard the clear voices of the Republican politicians. The majority of them would brook no compromise with the South and were arming their states for coercion.

The insistence of the governors increased after the new administration began. While Lincoln ignored the governors in distributing patronage, he could not dismiss their demands for action. The Fort Sumter expedition and the subsequent calls for troops, while not dictated by the governors, accorded with their demands. Yet , even as he took an action they demanded, Lincoln seized the initiative from the state political leaders. In the long run, national decisions had to be made by national officers, and Lincoln did not shirk the obligation. As he had advised Zachary Taylor to do, the president was prepared to say, or seem to say, "By the Eternal, I take the responsibility."

With the initiative in his hands, Lincoln moved to limit the influence of the governors. When, early in May, the governors of western states assembled in Cleveland to urge the administration to greater action and to outline demands for marching boldly to the Gulf of Mexico, Lincoln took them at their word and called for forty regiments of three-year volunteers. These were no state militia called by commanders-in-chief of state troops and loaned temporarily to the government, but federal soldiers subject to the laws of the United States. Without knowing it, or even realizing the political consequences of their acts, the governors raised the troops and commissioned the officers. But they were no longer commanders-in-chief; they were convenient recruiting officers for a growing national army. The generals owed their appointments to the president, and the colonels held their commissions at his pleasure. Lincoln had taken command.

Thereafter, the president and the federal government kept the governors busy with new duties. Moreover, to harass them, and to raise the specter of their loss of power, the war department authorized colonels to raise regiments in the states without reference to, and in competition with, the troops the governors were raising. The governors protested and won their point, but the government turned to permitting generals to recruit their own commands. John Andrew saw clearly the political implication of allowing Benjamin F. Butler to control the regiments he raised. He squabbled with Butler, and carried his case to Washington. It was symbolic of the declining power of the governors that he appealed where once he had directed. It was a greater symbol when he lost his appeal.

The efforts of the governors to recruit troops brought them increased difficulties both with the government and with their own constituents. Steadily they lost influence, and, with it, much of their political power. John Andrew and other governors, most of them abolitionists, seized upon the hope that they could force the administration to use Negro troops and at the same time advance the abolitionist cause. Andrew and others concocted an elaborate scheme—it really grew into the dimensions of a plot—to raise troops for an army to be commanded by Frémont which would set forth without reference to Lincoln's war to invade the South and arm slaves. To mature the plan, Andrew called the governors to a meeting at Altoona, Pennsylvania, on September 23, 1862. It was no coincidence that Lincoln chose the previous day to issue the preliminary Emancipation Proclamation. The proclamation was a masterstroke of politics, cutting the humanitarian ground from under the state politicians, and leaving them with only the alternative of applauding the president's acts.

Thereafter, both the prestige and the power of the governors ebbed. They had lost the power to direct war policy, lost control of troops as they became recruiting sergeants. Loss of prestige meant loss of political power, and by the elections of 1862 the governors had reason to fear they might be ousted from their offices. Democrats won control of legislatures, and put Horatio Seymour in the governor's chair in Albany. But, even as the state politicians were about to succumb to despair, Lincoln moved to their aid. In the Border States, he had used the army to control elections and to insure the establishment of loyal governments. In 1863 he moved with arbitrary arrests, soldiers at the polls, and soldiers sent home to vote, into the Northern States. In Ohio, Indiana, and Pennsylvania, troops patrolled the polls and insured the election of Republicans. In November 19, 1863, while Lincoln was speaking at Gettysburg, a regiment was supervising a special congressional election in nearby Delaware. By 1864 the troops were ready for political action. In a sufficient number of states to control the electoral college, the army turned the balance between Lincoln and McClellan. And with Lincoln's victory there went the election of the governors. In 1860 the governors, masters of the party in the states, had put Lincoln in the White House. In 1864 the man in the White House, with mastery over a national party, insured the election of the governors.

Building a national party, however, involved more than subordinating the politicians in the states. There were, in addition, the politicians in Congress, and with them Lincoln faced constantly the hated specter of state and national office. William Pitt Fessenden, Charles Sumner, Henry Wilson, Zachariah Chandler, Jacob Collamer, Lyman Trumbull, Benjamin F. Wade, and John P. Hale had long senatorial service behind them, while David Wilmot, John Sherman, and others had been in the House of Representatives. Two senators from Kansas, James H. Lane and Samuel C. Pomeroy, and two from Restored Virginia, John S. Carlile and Waitman Willey, were untried as senators, but fully experienced in the arts of politics. In the House, Galusha Grow, Thaddeus Stevens, John A. Bingham, James M. Ashley, Schuyler Colfax, George W. Julian, Elihu B. Washburn, Owen Lovejoy, and Justin Morrill were well known and time-tested politicians. They were superior in experience to Abraham Lincoln, who, as Sam Medary saw it, "most unfortunately for the country and his party, had never progressed farther in statesmanship than is learned in the pleasant position of county court practice where wit and wisdom reign more for the amusement of the thing than to *settle* great state questions."

With such political talent in the legislature, Lincoln made no effort to assume leadership in legislation. He had, indeed, no legislative program to promote, and faced none of the problems of the legislative leader who needed to bargain and cajole, to coerce and to compromise to get support for a bill. On the other hand, he had a war to conduct and needed the support of an integrated national party to bring it to a successful conclusion. But here he met discordant factions, differing from one another on the purpose of the war, the manner in which it should be fought, and on the results to be obtained. Here he met conciliators who would bargain with the South, moderates who wished to conduct the war with as little social and economic disturbance as possible, and radicals who wished to effect a drastic reorganization of American society at its end.

Fully aware of the contending factions, Lincoln delayed calling Congress into session until four months after his inauguration. Democrats charged then, and the echo has reverberated for a century, that Lincoln precipitated a war in order to save and consolidate the Republican Party. Whatever his purpose, his act gave the party a program and brought conciliators and compromisers among the politicians into line. Moreover, as the people of the North rushed to the mass meetings—and some to the regiments—the politicians could read the signs. "Mr. Lincoln judged wisely" in delaying the assembling of Congress, thought James G. Blaine. "Time was needed for the growth and consolidation of Northern opinion, and that senators and representatives, after the full development of patriotic feeling in the free states, would meet in a frame of mind better suited to the discharge of the weighty duties devolving upon them."

In addition to the desire to use public pressure on the politicians, Lincoln had, in Blaine's opinion, another reason for delaying the assembling of Congress. Kentucky's congressmen had not yet been chosen, and the President desired to "give ample time for canvassing" for the special election on June 20. In the canvass, recounted Blaine, Lincoln "did everything therefore that he could properly do, to aid Kentucky in reaching a conclusion favorable to the Union." In the view of Democrats, who used none of Blaine's mealy-mouthed ver-

bosity to describe the situation, Lincoln went beyond the bounds of propriety in aiding Kentucky. General Jeremiah T. Boyle arrested citizens on the eve of election, and troops at the polls discouraged Democratic voters. The results were heartening to Lincoln. Nine out of Kentucky's ten congressmen were Unionists who could be grateful to Lincoln for their success.

The combination of popular pressure and direct aid, illustrated in the first months of the administration, frequently proved effective devices for dealing with the politicians in Congress. They were not, however, always available to Lincoln. The radical faction, too, used the Union Leagues and the propaganda agencies of the Union League clubs to build up popular pressure for their policies. Moreover, the radicals controlled the Congressional Committee on the Conduct of the War which was at once an investigating body, a fountain-head of radical propaganda, and a pressure group seeking to direct war policy.

With these factional groups Lincoln had to deal. Frequently he found himself forced to yield. Whatever the military merits of George B. McClellan may have been, political necessity demanded his removal from command. Less able and less successful generals—Benjamin Butler and Nathaniel Banks, for example—whose political views were more acceptable to the vociferous radical clique, remained long in command. Whatever the humanitarian or diplomatic advantages of the Emancipation Proclamation may have been, its issuance and its timing constituted a yielding to the politicians in state and national capitols.

Yet, Abraham Lincoln was not the pliant tool of the radical faction. He yielded to political necessity, but he was apt in evading the demands of the politicians and ingenious in diverting them. He handled the Chase-Seward imbroglio in his cabinet with dexterity, took advantage of the premature announcement of Chase's hopes in the Pomeroy Circular, and released Chase from his cabinet after the political danger was passed. He used state legislators and Montgomery Blair's corps of postmasters to launch a "grass roots" demand for his own renomination. He bargained for Frémont's removal during the campaign of 1864. He was a master politician, using the patronage, the army, the ability to appeal to the people over the heads of the politicians, and a shrewd capacity to bargain to build a national party and to keep rival politicians from open and overt revolt.

His most serious problem, and his nearest defeat came on the issues of reconstruction. His plans were many, and each was political in orientation and looked to the eventual establishment of proper practical relations between the seceded states and the national government. Beginning with the Border States, where Lincoln fostered Unionist parties and encouraged the replacement of disloyal governors, his program developed through the establishment of military governors to the eventual announcement of a full-blown Proclamation of Amnesty and Reconstruction. From the beginning, Democratic critics pointed out that Lincoln's plans were political and designed to create a personal party, supported by the army. In the opinion of the Columbus *Crisis,* all of Lincoln's acts revealed "settled designs upon the rights of the states and the liberties of the people." Certainly, Lincoln had no program for restoring the old rights of the states or of restoring the *old* federal union. He was waging a war against the states, and was building a national party. He watched patiently while Andrew Johnson labored in Tennessee to create a political party before he

tried to restore the machinery of government. He gave free reign to Butler and Banks in New Orleans as they sought for a loyal nucleus about which to gather a party.

When Lincoln issued his proclamation of Amnesty and Reconstruction in December, 1863, the Democrats were quick to see its political significance. "As a party manifesto," pronounced the New York *World,* "it is a creditable specimen of political dexterity. It trims with marvelous dexterity between the two factions of the Republican party." It was, in fact, "Mr. Lincoln's trump card for the presidential nomination." Other Democrats were more apt in spelling out the details, and soon they were counting the number of voters who would be needed to carry the states of the South. The movement, said the *World,* was not "discreditable to Mr. Lincoln's shrewdness as a politician. . . . There could not be a shrewder device for enabling President Lincoln to re-elect himself." The one-tenth who would take the "abolition oath" would cast the electoral votes of the Southern states. When a military expedition went off to Florida, the *World* saw the movement was not military, but political: "The object was to make it a rotten-borough state under the amnesty proclamation, so that it could throw its electoral vote for Mr. Lincoln."

The radical politicians of Congress hardly needed instruction from the Democrats on the political meaning of the Amnesty Proclamation. Long had they favored a program of conquest which would insure far-reaching social and economic changes in the South. They approved Ben Butler's harsh regime in New Orleans as they saw him destroying the Southern economic system and organizing a new electorate. They approved the social experiments in the Sea Islands of Carolina where the army, treasury officials, and agents of humanitarian societies quarrelled with each other as they sought to combine a reorganization of society with the production of cotton. They saw, as quickly as the Democrats, that Lincoln's plans embodied the personal control over the Southern states. When congressmen from a reconstructed government in Arkansas arrived in Washington, radical Henry Winter Davis denounced Lincoln's proclamation as "a grave usurpation upon the legislative authority of the people." Soon Davis had ready a bill for a more complicated process of reconstruction than Lincoln contemplated, and the members of Congress turned to denouncing Lincoln and his schemes. In the Senate, where reconstruction policies were a constant subject of debate, the Davis bill received a little specific attention. The final passage of the Wade-Davis Bill was done with so little enthusiasm that Lincoln had no hesitancy in giving it a pocket veto and accompanying it with a fresh declaration of his own policy.

Radicals Wade and Davis issued a "manifesto" denouncing presidential usurpation, and thereafter, until the end of his life, the radical politicians harassed Lincoln on the issues of reconstruction. The election of 1864 brought success to the Republicans without recourse to the electoral votes of the "rotten-borough" states, and in the congressional session of 1864-65, Charles Sumner filibustered against the recognition of a reconstructed government in Louisiana. On the issue, Lincoln was forced to retreat, and he spent his last weeks devising new schemes of reconstruction. The new schemes never matured, and Andrew Johnson inherited the problem and faced the determined and well-organized politicians of congress.

The end was inconclusive. Lincoln had, indeed, built a national party. He had used the patronage, the prestige of his position, the army, and skillful popular appeals to subordinate the state parties and mold them into national unity. He had had less success in combatting factionalism at the national level, had not succeeded in winning undisputed control over the party he had created. He might, indeed, have recalled his early definition of politicians as "a set of men who have interests aside from the interests of the people, and who, to say the most of them, are taken as a mass, at least one long step removed from honest men." And, had he remembered this, he might also have recalled, as he surveyed his own substantial accomplishments, that he had also added—"being a politician myself . . ."

T. HARRY WILLIAMS (b. 1909), professor of history at Louisiana State University, in writing *Lincoln and the Radicals* (1941) entitled the first chapter "A House Divided." The house was not the American nation but the Republican party. The reader should be alert to Williams' analysis of Republican factions, his description of the Radicals, and his statement of their aims, motives, and methods. Of special importance are the relationship he depicts between Lincoln and the Radicals and his view of the outcome of that relationship.*

T. Harry Williams

Lincoln Surrenders to the Radicals

On a warm June night in 1862 an impassioned orator stood before a New York audience at Cooper Union, "the nation's forum." He was analyzing the radical and conservative factions in the Republican Party that were struggling for the mastery of the administration of Abraham Lincoln. Owen Lovejoy of Illinois belonged to the radical faith. Zealous, fiery, the Calvinist minister in politics, hating slavery since a mob had murdered his abolitionist brother twenty-five years before, he had prophesied in the House of Representatives long before the Civil War that the slaves would walk to emancipation as the children of Israel had journeyed to the Promised Land, "through the *Red* Sea." Now he faced his metropolitan listeners, a Jeremiah from the Western prairies, to denounce those moderate, conservative elements in the Republican organization whose influence prevented Lincoln from converting the war against the Southern Confederacy into a holy crusade for the destruction of slavery. "The President," cried Lovejoy, "is like a man driving a horse in the thills of a buggy, and leading another behind him by the halter-strap. The one in the shafts is a most superb animal—broad between the eyes, ears small, short around the throat, stifle full and hard, short coupled, and can clear ditch and hedge, high spirited and fast." This was the radical steed, eager to pull driver and buggy along the road of freedom, but it was held back by the conservative horse

*From T. Harry Williams, *Lincoln and the Radicals* (Madison, Wis.: University of Wisconsin Press, 1941), pp. 3–18, by permission of the copyright owners, the Regents of the University of Wisconsin. Footnotes omitted.

in the rear, a miserable, awkward, lagging beast. Lincoln contributed to the creeping progress of the vehicle by reining in the champing creature in front, because he too was slow and cautious. But, concluded Lovejoy, "If he does not drive as fast as I would, he is on the right road, and it is only a question of time."

More than a year before, in Boston, another product of Calvinism in politics, Wendell Phillips, the eloquent voice of New England abolitionism, spoke in similar scornful terms of the president he had supported in the election of 1860 and the conservatives in the Republican Party. At Tremont Temple, packed with his tumultuous followers, Phillips castigated Lincoln for his seeming intention to conduct the government without striking a vigorous blow at slavery, and predicted, "A pawn on the political chessboard, his value is in his position; with fair effort, we may soon change him for knight, bishop, or queen, and sweep the board." The Republican Party had timidly undertaken the solution of the slavery problem, he said, but the drift of events and the pressure of the radicals would force it to champion complete emancipation and political equality for the liberated slaves. Phillips' forecast was amazingly accurate. Lincoln remained a harried figure on the chessboard, but the radicals captured all the pieces. Years later, near the close of the war, Phillips exultingly referred to the victorious consummation of the radical program despite conservative opposition: "the administration has wished, many times, but has been unable to resist the Revolution. It has overborne them."

No polyglot army of an ancient emperor ever exhibited more variety than did the Republican Party in 1860. Within its diverse ranks were radicals and abolitionists who wanted to destroy every vestige of slavery, moderates who would have been content to restrict its expansion into the territories, Whigs, Free-Soilers, and antislavery Democrats, Eastern manufacturers who hoped for a protective tariff and Western farmers who favored free trade, hardened machine politicians and visionary reformers. Two threads of unity bound this heterogeneous coalition into the semblance of a national organization. Each constituent part was opposed, although with varying intensity, to the institution of Negro slavery. And the party broadly represented the social ideology of the "free," capitalistic society of the North, whose ruling middle class felt it must strike down the political power of the slavocracy in order to complete its economic control of the nation.

There was a right and a left wing in the party even before 1860. The moderates were typified by Lincoln, the courtly Orville H. Browning of Illinois, James R. Doolittle of Wisconsin, and Vermont's venerable Jacob Collamer. They advocated the gradual extinction of slavery, compensated emancipation, and colonization of the Negroes in another land. They detested slavery, and believed the institution could not survive the strain of a long civil war. But they also feared and distrusted the revolutionary ardor of the radicals and the spirit of fanaticism that was inherent in the abolitionists. They opposed the wartime abolition of slavery except as a final measure of military necessity to prevent the disruption of the Union. Hence the conservatives fought from the beginning the hasty plans of the radicals to bring about immediate emancipation. Temperamentally they objected to the reforming zeal of the radicals. Furthermore, unlike the abolitionists, they had some appreciation of the practical difficulties that would follow the sudden liberation of several million slaves. The conservatives were reasonable, able men, but their very virtues rendered them incapable of coping with the determined radicals in a revolutionary period. In contrast to the radicals, the moderates were negative and vacillating, lacking a cohesive program of consistent action.

The radicals were the real driving power in the party. They were the men whom young John Hay, Lincoln's secretary, who had encountered their fierce prototypes of the French Revolution in his superficial reading, dubbed the Jacobins. Aggressive, vindictive, and narrowly sectional, the radicals hated slavery with a bitter personal feeling. But more than slavery they hated its political representatives, the proud cavaliers who had dominated Congress in the fifties and who had scourged the sputtering radical minority with polished gibes. Unlike many of the moderates, the Jacobins welcomed the outbreak of civil war as the longed-for opportunity to destroy slavery and to drive the "slave traders" from the national temple. In 1861 they had opposed attempts at compromise which might have averted secession. Conciliation of the sections would have deprived the Republican Party of its excuse for being; would, thought Michigan's Zachariah Chandler, "rupture" the organization. Chandler worked vigorously against compromise, and calmly welcomed the holocaust: "Without a little blood-letting, this Union will not . . . be worth a rush!" The radicals stood for instant emancipation, the confiscation of "rebel" property, the use of colored soldiers, civil and, when it should become expedient, political equality for the Negro. They loved the Negro less for himself than as an instrument with which they might fasten Republican political and economic control upon the South. Closely associated with the Jacobins, but more sincerely radical, were the abolitionists. Fanat-ical and impractical, their motto was that of all revolutionaries, "Let there be justice even though the heavens crumble." The abolitionists, within yet beyond the party, often forced the radical politicos to adopt a more extreme position than the exigencies of the moment warranted.

The Jacobins were led by master politicians. In the House of Representatives, caustic, terrifying, clubfooted old Thaddeus Stevens ran the Republican machine, hurling his devastating taunts equally at Democrats, Republican laggards, the president, and "the vile ingredient called conservatism, which is worse than secessionism." In the Senate the radical leaders were Ohio's "Bluff Ben" Wade, endowed with a brutal wit, who had first won fame by offering to meet the Southern hotspurs upon the field of honor with squirrel rifles at thirty paces as the weapons; grim, furious Zack Chandler, "Xanthippe in pants," who bossed Michigan politics with an iron hand and a liberal supply of liquor; and Charles Sumner of Massachusetts, handsome, scholarly, and humorless, despised by many radicals for his cant, but valued as an impressive show-window display.

There were economic as well as political factions in the party, but the fissures of separation were narrower here. The Northern bourgeoisie sought through the Republican organization to complete "the industrial revolution" by wresting political power from the slavocracy, and for this class the party horoscope forecast fat rewards. To the owners of the spindles, the looms, and the iron furnaces of the Northeast, it promised a protective tariff. To business in general it offered a national banking system controlled by the financial interests, government subsidies for the construction of railroads, and free access to the rich resources of the public domain. To less fortunate members of the middle class and to the Northwestern farmers plagued by inadequate transportation facilities, it held forth the hope of free homesteads and federal aid for the improvement of rivers and harbors and for the building of railroads and canals. Eastern nabobs and Western agrarians might quarrel, as they did immediately after the war, over the tariff, but in 1860 they closed their ranks against a common foe, the planter aristocrats.[1]

No one better expressed the Republican ideal of a competitive capitalistic society, with freedom of economic opportunity for the middle class, disenthralled from the dominance of a feudal aristocracy, than did Abraham Lincoln as he analyzed the issues of the war in his first message to Congress. "This is essentially a people's contest," he said. "On the side of the Union it is a struggle for maintaining in the world that form and substance of government whose leading object is to elevate the condition of men—to lift artificial weights from all shoulders; to clear the paths of laudable pursuit for all; to afford all an unfettered start, and a fair chance in the race of life."

Senator John Sherman of industrial Ohio phrased the economic objectives of his party more bluntly: "We know very well that the great objects which those who elected Mr. Lincoln expect him to accomplish will be to secure to free labor its just right to the Territories of the United States; to protect, as far as practicable, by wise revenue laws, the labor of our people; to secure the public lands to actual settlers, instead of to non-resident speculators; to develop the internal resources of the country by opening new means of communication between the Atlantic and the Pacific."

But the conquering bourgeoisie intended to do more than use their new-fledged political power to consolidate an already dominant economic position. They meant also to extend the new industrial order to the South and make that section an economic adjunct of the North. A "free" capitalistic Dixie would mean a richer market for Northern factories, untapped investment opportunities for Yankee entrepreneurs, and ideological re-enforcements for the protective tariff. Those roseate anticipations could not be realized without first destroying slavery. John Sherman pictured for his Senate colleagues the tempting possibilities of an industrialized South unhampered by slave labor:

When I look upon those deep bays, those fertile fields, requiring only energetic labor to develop them, when I see those marts of commerce in the very center of our Atlantic coast, I wonder in amazement that a million of men are not now crowded there, delving and striking and working with honest toil for an honest reward. . . . But, sir, there is no other cause [for this lack of development] except simply that labor . . . which has built up New York, New England, and the West, is there degraded by the presence of slaves.

Representative J. K. Moorhead, a henchman of the Pennsylvania iron masters, declared that slavery hindered the material development of the South, that if Kentucky freed her slaves she could develop her iron resources and she would then join Pennsylvania in advocacy of the tariff. "We would have more labor for the laboring men of the country, and we would develop the resources of the country more

[1] The Republicans enacted most of their economic program into law during the war: the Morrill tariff, the Homestead Act, subsidies for the transcontinental railroads, and the establishment of the national bank system. Differences within the party grew out of disputes as to whether real or personal property should bear the burden of war taxation. Representative Sydney Edgerton of Ohio attacked one of Stevens' revenue bills because it bore heavily upon agriculture and favored "the great stockholders, the money lenders, and the merchant princes of Wall street, and all the great capitalists." *Congressional Globe,* 37 Congress, 1 Session, 282. See *ibid,* 325–326, for similar remarks by Isaac N. Arnold of Illinois.

fully than we have ever done." The Republican plans for the economic renova-
tion of the South envisioned a social revolution which would elevate the Negroes
and poorer whites to the top of the political pile. Thus a Southern bourgeoisie
would displace the ruling landed aristocracy, to make doubly sure that in the nation the Republican Party and the forces
of industrial capitalism would retain the
favored position they had won in 1860.
Wendell Phillips frankly stated the Republican design for the new South when
federal troops occupied Louisiana in 1863.
"The whole social system of the Gulf states
is to be taken to pieces; every bit of it."

Almost from the day when armed conflict began, the radical and conservative
factions clashed over the purposes of the
war. Lincoln and the moderates attempted
to make the restoration of the Union the
sole objective; and they would have restored it, if possible, without at the same
time destroying slavery. Senator Browning,
who often acted as Lincoln's spokesman,
asserted in July, 1861: "For one, I should
rejoice to see all the States in rebellion return to their allegiance; and if they return,
if they lay down the arms of their rebellion
and come back to their duties and their
obligations, they will be as fully protected,
now and at all times hereafter, as they
have ever been before, in all their rights,
including the ownership, use, and management of slaves."

In the president's mind, the preservation
of the American experiment in government overshadowed all other questions. He
regarded emancipation as incidental to
this larger issue, to be resorted to as a last
desperate measure, and then to be initiated by himself as an exercise of the war
powers of the executive rather than by
Congress. His intense conviction that secession must be crushed at all costs even im-

pelled him to throw overboard considerations of party regularity. By inviting
Northern Democrats and Border State
slaveholders to accept prominent positions
in the administration, he endeavored to
enlarge the Republican organization into
an all-inclusive Union party, a "popular
front" whose one resolution was to end the
war quickly and re-establish the nation.

Against this mild program the Jacobins
inveighed, ranted, and sneered. Many of
them felt that Lincoln was only a well-
meaning incompetent who lacked the
"inclination to put down this rebellion
with the strong hand required." The radicals were determined that the war must not
end without the death of slavery. "We
cannot afford to go over this ground more
than once," wrote aristocratic Charles
Francis Adams of Massachusetts. "The
slave question must be settled this time
once for all." Impetuous George W. Julian,
leader of the Indiana radicals, exclaimed
that the war would be "an empty mockery
of our sufferings and sacrifices" if slavery
were spared. "Bluff Ben" Wade declared
that if the conflict "continues thirty years
and bankrupts the whole nation, I hope to
God there will be no peace until we can
say there is not a slave in this land." The
fervid outbursts of radicals like Julian and
Wade against the president's policy were
dictated by coolheaded consideration of
political expediency. If after a short war
the Southern states returned to the Union
with the institution of slavery still intact
and the political control of the slaveholders
unshaken, Republican influence in the government would be nullified and the economic revolution vexatiously delayed. A
victory achieved upon Lincoln's plan, protested frank Martin Conway of Kansas,
"must inevitably result in restoring the
domination of the slaveholding class," and
hence could "bring no lasting peace."
"What!" cried a Western radical, "bring

back the rebel States, into full fellowship as members of the union, with their full delegations in both Houses of Congress. They, with the pro-slavery conservatives of the Border States and the Democrats of the Northern states, will control Congress. Republicans and Republican principles will be in the minority and under law, and this latter state would be worse than the former—worse than war itself."

In contrast to the administration's "sickly policy of an inoffensive war," as Julian termed it, the Jacobins demanded a line of action "suited to remorseless and revolutionary violence." The magnetic Senator Edward Baker, who was later to lose his life leading a rash charge at the battle of Ball's Bluff, proclaimed in 1861 a war of subjugation against the seceded states: "We may have to reduce them to the condition of Territories, and send from Massachusetts or from Illinois Governors to control them." Owen Lovejoy grimly predicted, "If there is no other way to quell this rebellion, we will make a solitude, and call it peace." Blunt John Hickman of Pennsylvania threatened that the conquest of the Confederacy would "leave the track of the chariot wheels of war so deep on the southern soil that a century may not obliterate it," and Zachariah Chandler, expressing the fierce, intolerant wartime spirit of the radicals, proclaimed, "A rebel has sacrificed all his rights. He has no right to life, liberty, property, or the pursuit of happiness. Everything you give him, even life itself, is a boon which he has forfeited."

Always a step before the foremost, Thaddeus Stevens was willing that the South "be laid waste, and made a desert," and "repeopled by a band of freemen." He told a Republican convention in Pennsylvania: "Abolition—yes! Abolish everything on the face of the earth but this Union; free every slave—slay every traitor—burn every rebel mansion, if these things be nec-

essary to preserve this temple of freedom to the world and to our posterity." The sardonic old man observed to a young friend in the army, "I infer your duties lie at some distance from the rebels. It were a pity to hurt those that our Government treats so tenderly." [2]

If the Jacobins could not have their remorseless, revolutionary war, they were not sure that they wanted any at all. The vociferous John P. Hale of New Hampshire, shouting in the Senate at the beginning of hostilities, "This is the day; this is the hour; this is the time; this is the experiment," declared boldly, "If we cannot put down this rebellion, let them put us down." Even John Sherman, who was not an out-and-out radical, said, "For me, I am for a war that will either establish or overthrow the government. ... We need such a war, and we have it now." Holding this uncompromising attitude, the radicals found it difficult, if not impossible, to support the administration's efforts to bring the war to a rapid conclusion without destroying slavery. They believed that if the struggle continued long enough, public opinion would force the government to resort to emancipation and the arming of the slaves. Hence they favored a policy that would prolong the war until they had sufficient control of the party to force the radical program upon the reluctant Lincoln. "And we don't want" the war "to be hurried," wrote Horace Greeley, the white-haired sage of the *New York Tribune*, "but to be earnestly carried on to a righteous conclusion."

---

[2] See S. Fish to Lyman Trumbull, June 25, 1861, in the Trumbull MSS., advocating that the South be taught "a bloody lesson," which it would remember for "a thousand generations"; Trumbull to M. C. Lea, November 5, 1861, in White, *Trumbull,* 171–172, in which Senator Trumbull said, "War means desolation, and they who have brought it on must be made to feel all its horrors."

Their insistence upon the necessity of a long war placed the radicals in the embarrassing, and often sinister, position of regarding Union defeats on the battlefield as helpful to their cause. Congressman Charles Sedgwick of New York said, "We ought to be whipped into that humble frame of mind which will make us willing to get soldiers of any color, and enlist them without scruple even in the enemy's country." From Wendell Phillips came the prayer, "God grant us so many reverses that the government may learn its duty." The Olympian Charles Sumner, so detached from individuals that he could ignore the fate of the common soldier in his zeal for radicalism, exclaimed:

I fear our victories more than our defeats. There must be more delay and more suffering—yet another "plague" before all will agree to "let my people go"; and the war cannot, must not, end till then. . . . We are too victorious. . . . If the rebellion should suddenly collapse, Democrats, copperheads, and Seward would insist upon amnesty and the Union, and "no question asked about slavery." God save us from any such calamity! . . . Before this comes, I wish two hundred thousand negroes with muskets in their hands, and then I shall not fear compromise.

At the end of the war that ardent feminine radical L. Maria Child ascribed much of the success of the Jacobin program to the military disasters suffered by the federal armies:

If we had had thorough, conscientious rulers, in cabinet and field, the war would have been brought to a close so soon that we, in the pride of quick success, should have shoved aside the black man, as of no account in the settlement of our difficulties. Had it not been for reiterated calls upon our sons to fill the ranks of the army, popular opinion would never have sanctioned the arming of the negroes; and the present feeling in favor of emancipation is largely owing to the fact that *their* blood has been shed to spare *ours*.

All this is not to say that the Jacobins conspired for the defeat of the military forces in order to further their political designs. It simply means that they felt no enthusiasm for a war that did not include as one of its inevitable results the destruction of slavery. Rather than see the South brought back into the Union with slavery still in existence, most radicals would have preferred that the nation remain permanently divided. But as they slowly compelled Lincoln to adopt the radical policies, the Jacobins became increasingly vigorous in their support of the war.

The Jacobins demanded of the administration not only that it prosecute the war to a righteous conclusion but that it commit the management of the conflict to unadulterated radicals. For this reason they bitterly resented Lincoln's attempt to convert the party organization into a broad-bottomed coalition of all the elements in the loyal states who would support a war for the Union, and his consequent bestowal of high civil and military offices upon Democrats and conservatives who supported his program. They feared that the inclusion of these extraneous groups in the government would smother their own influence and vitiate the party's opposition to slavery. Furthermore, if Democratic and conservative generals and politicians should prove to be the great heroes of the war, they would also inherit the lush political offices after the peace, thus dooming the radicals to the cheerless existence of a frustrated minority. An alert Indiana editor, sensing Lincoln's intention of constructing an all-parties government even before he assumed the presidency, asked Julian, "Is there not a movement . . . to build up a 'union party' in the north which shall absorb Americans and Douglas men, and Conservative Republicans; done for the purpose of killing what they term the Abolition element in the Republican party, aimed at men of our Stamp. The movement cannot amount to anything unless it should be the disruption of the Republican party." John Sherman blamed Lincoln's procedure for the Republican losses in the elections of 1862: "The Republican organization was voluntarily abandoned by the president and his leading followers, and a no-party Union was formed." If the Republicans, advised Sherman, "have the wisdom to throw overboard the old débris that joined them in the Union movement, they will succeed. If not, they are doomed." Joshua R. Giddings, veteran foe of slavery and political godfather of Wade and Julian, thought that the president, by bringing into the party groups which could unite only upon a single issue, handicapped it with a platform that was too narrow to appeal to large numbers of voters, and condemned it to enter every campaign "without doctrines, principles or character." This, said Giddings, must inevitably result in the disintegration of the party.

Upon the Democrats in Lincoln's popular front the angry radicals placed the onus for the administration's delay in taking an aggressive antislavery position. The president, wooing the support of the Democracy, appointed receptive members of that party to positions of power and influence: George B. McClellan, Don Carlos Buell, and Henry W. Halleck, in the army; and in the Cabinet, former Democrats Montgomery Blair and Gideon Welles. He braved the ire of the Republican spoilsmen, avid for the prizes of victory, by refusing to purge the government bureaus and departments of their Democratic incumbents, thus ignoring "the wholesome rule" that "no one who does not believe enthusiastically in the war should have a place." The Jacobins charged that the entire bureaucracy was shot through with Democratic treason, with the result, said John Sherman, that "there have been constant impediments thrown in the way of the organization of our military forces." Disgusted radicals like the pompous Salmon P. Chase thought that the misguided president was entrusting the direction of the war "almost exclusively to his political opponents." Democratic ascendancy, complained George W. Julian, was responsible for the administration's stand against emancipation and its policy of a milk-and-water war. "To this strange deference to slavery must be referred the fact that such swarms of disloyal men have been retained in the several departments of the government, and that the spirit and energy of the war have been paralyzed from the beginning."

If Democratic prominence in the civil offices disturbed the Jacobins, Democratic domination of the army infuriated them. Partly because of Lincoln's patronage policy and more because of the previous convictions of most regular army men, Democratic officers controlled both the important and the subordinate commands in the early period of the war. Henry Wilson asserted in the Senate in 1861 that of the one hundred and ten brigadier generals in the army, eighty were Democrats. "Whenever there is a separate command," he deplored, "with but one solitary exception, that command is under the control of a general opposed to the present Administration." Julian estimated that four fifths of the major and brigadier generals were Democrats. The radicals suspected that the Democratic masters of the army nourished a sympathy for slavery that bordered on treason, and that the "infernal hold-back pro-slavery" philosophy of the military chieftains prevented a vigorous prosecution of the war. Martin Conway claimed that there was not "more than one sincere abolitionist or emancipationist among the military authorities," and Joseph Medill of the *Chicago Tribune* sneered at the "scores of luke warm, half secession officers in command who cannot bear to strike a blow lest it hurt their rebel friends or jeopardize the precious protectors of slavery." In the place of conservative West Pointers the Jacobins demanded "generals with ideas," who on the battlefield would be "almost irresistible because swayed by the great invisible forces."

So long as Democrats and conservatives occupied the positions of power in the government, the radicals believed that it was bootless for them to force the president to issue an emancipation edict. "Of what use would such a proclamation be," asked Wendell Phillips, "if conservatives or Democrats in the army and Cabinet enforced it? If the President should proclaim emancipation and Halleck and McClellan and Buell smother it under pretence of executing the measure, it will prove a failure." Consequently the implacable radicals insisted that all parties other than their own be expelled from the popular front. "We demand," said Phillips, "a proclamation of freedom, war on war principles to be conducted by such men as Sumner, Stevens, and Wade, and their friends in the Cabinet, and by Hunter, Sigel, and Fremont in the field. . . . No emancipation policy is of any value unless its earnest and down-right friends are put at the head of affairs."

Against Lincoln and his conservative program the Jacobins waged a winning battle. Both logic and time aided their cause. For Lincoln proposed the impossible—to conduct the war for the preservation of the status quo which had produced the war. The radicals, before the end of the struggle, had gutted his policies almost completely. They forced the adoption of emancipation as one of the objectives of the war. They pushed through measures providing for the employment of Negro soldiers and for the confiscation of the property of "rebels." They drove the Democratic generals from the army and weakened conservative influence in the Cabinet. They defeated Lincoln's attempt to control the process of reconstruction by refusing congressional recognition for his state governments in the South. At the close of the war the radicals, like Hamlet, looked at a political cemetery littered with dead but victorious issues, each the skull of a poor Yorick that once had been a live and burning contention.

The wily Lincoln surrendered to the conquering Jacobins in every controversy before they could publicly inflict upon him a damaging reverse. Like the fair Lucretia threatened with ravishment, he averted his fate by instant compliance. In 1865 L. Maria Child observed, perhaps ironically, "I think we have reason to thank God for Abraham Lincoln. With all his deficiencies," he had been a man "who was willing to grow."

A leader of the Radicals in the United States Senate was
Benjamin F. Wade of Ohio, chairman of the Joint
Committee on the Conduct of the War. His biographer,
HANS L. TREFOUSSE (b. 1921), professor of history at
Brooklyn College, undertakes a general reassessment of the
committee. Note the questions he sets out to re-examine
and the answers he provides. His conclusions may be
compared with those of Williams. Note in particular
Trefousse's interpretation of Lincoln's response to the
committee's influence. In *The Radical Republicans; Lincoln's
Vanguard for Racial Justice* (1969), Trefousse expands his
reassessment.*

Hans L. Trefousse

The Radical Committee
Had No Power

Over one hundred years have passed
since Congress established the Joint Committee on the Conduct of the War. Fierce-
ly attacked when it first began to take
testimony, the committee has generally
been treated critically ever since. Contemporaries called it a "sort of Aulic Council"
and characterized it as "a mischievous organization which assumed dictatorial powers." More recent observers have made
similar charges. They have accused it of
having "arrogated the right to make affirmative decisions," have criticized it for
wielding "inquisitorial powers," and have
charged it with the loss "of thousands of
lives" because of unwarranted interference
with the military.

Since it was largely dominated by Radicals whose historiographical standing soon
reached a nadir, the committee has generally been considered a terrible handicap
to Lincoln, a vicious engine of political
persecution, and a dangerous precedent for
congressional interference. Not even William W. Pierson's perceptive article on the
subject in 1918 reversed this trend of
thought, and no further important work
was done in the field until the appearance
of T. Harry Williams' doctoral dissertation
in 1937. In this excellent survey, supple-
mented by an article two years later, the
author stressed the differences between
Lincoln and the committee and its importance as a propaganda agency, themes
which prevailed in his subsequent book,
Lincoln and the Radicals. Nevertheless, the
overall view of the committee as a dangerous meddler persisted, and when Sena-

*Hans L. Trefousse, "The Joint Committee on the Conduct of the War: A Reassessment," *Civil War History,*
X (March, 1964), 5–19. Footnotes omitted.

tor Harry S. Truman commenced a congressional investigation during World War II, he made a deliberate effort to avoid the alleged errors of his predecessors. Having been influenced by Douglas Southall Freeman, he believed that the Civil War body had been "of material assistance to the Confederacy." Thus had the traditional view been fully accepted.

What was the true role of the committee? What, if any, contributions did it make to the final success of the national cause? Was it really as unscrupulous as some observers have thought? Were its methods actually those of an inquisition, a court of the star chamber? And did it possess the vast powers that have been ascribed to it? These questions all seem to merit re-examination.

When the Joint Committee was established on December 10, 1861, it was empowered "to inquire into the conduct of the present war." Consisting of three members of the Senate and four Representatives, it could "send for persons and papers, and sit during the sessions of either House of Congress." After 1864, it was also given power to investigate war contracts and expenditures, and from time to time Congress commissioned it to conduct specific examinations of various subjects. As has been repeatedly pointed out, the committee was cosponsored by Radicals and conservatives, but because the chairman and the leading members were Radicals, it was soon identified with the extremist branch of the Republican party and became its principal agency of pressure and propaganda. As a legislative committee, however, it never possessed executive powers; while it could make recommendations and suggestions, it could not, by itself, appoint or dismiss officers of the armed forces.

That the committee took its work seriously is beyond doubt. Its chairman, Ben-

jamin F. Wade of Ohio, was an old antislavery leader who had tilted many a lance in the Senate with the defenders of the peculiar institution. Famous for his courage as well as his sarcasm, he was industrious, well-informed, and fanatically anxious to get on with the war. The same was true of his friend and colleague, Zachariah Chandler of Michigan, who had expressed an opinion, early in 1861, that "without a little blood letting, this Union will not . . . be worth a rush." The third original Senate member, Andrew Johnson, was at that time so bitter about his Southern enemies that, if anything, he exceeded his colleagues in zeal.

The House members were equally determined. George Washington Julian, who eventually married Joshua Giddings' daughter, conceived of himself as Giddings' political heir and never deviated from the stern principles which had made him the vice-presidential candidate on the Independent Democrats' ticket in 1852. John Covode was closely tied to the Radicals, and Daniel Gooch of Massachusetts, reputedly a conservative Republican, soon fell under his colleagues' spell. The last member, Moses Odell, was a Democrat from Brooklyn, but his actions were soon as determined as those of any Republican.

Possibly because of their radicalism and because of their desire to function effectively, the members decided to hold their meetings in secret. In their room in the capitol basement they ceaselessly interrogated contractors, public officials, and military personnel of all ranks, seeking reasons for failure and delay and ferreting out corruption and inefficiency.

In carrying out these activities, the members were able to achieve a number of real successes. First and foremost, they sought to remove conservative generals from active command, especially George B. McClellan and his supporters. Consid-

ering the conservatives constitutionally incapable of waging the type of aggressive
war deemed essential for victory, the committee held lengthy hearings and put considerable pressure upon the administration
to revamp the command structure. Lincoln
was by no means indifferent to these demands. Dubious about McClellan's abilities himself, the President first forced the
general to commit himself to some plan of
operation, then saw to it that his orders
were obeyed. When McClellan failed to
produce the desired results, Lincoln finally
decided to dismiss him. Those who believe
that the failure of the Peninsular campaign was due to the withholding of
McDowell's corps and Blenker's division
have naturally held the committee responsible for these decisions. The President,
however, was just as determined to secure
the defenses of Washington as the committee, and whether the added troops
would have enabled the cautious commander to take Richmond in 1862 may justly
be doubted. Indubitably, the committee's
hearings and stormy requests strengthened
the President's hand against the popular
general whose dismissal was essential if vigorous tactics were ever to be employed.

Second, the members were generally
committed to an all-out war effort which
included the abolition of slavery as soon as
possible. In pursuing this goal they worked
individually and collectively, sought to
gather supporting evidence, and harassed
the administration. Again, they were not
unsuccessful. Congress abolished slavery in
the territories and the District of Columbia
in the spring of 1862; Lincoln issued his
Emancipation Proclamation on January 1,
1863; and, on January 31, 1865, the requi-
site two-thirds majority passed the Thirteenth Amendment. By its hearings, entreaties, and propaganda, the committee had
contributed materially to these accomplishments.

Third, the group succeeded in uncover-
ing corruption and inefficiency. It held
hearings to probe unsystematic methods of
evacuating the wounded, abuses connected
with permits to trade with the enemy,
laxity in the paymaster's department,
lapses of security, failures in naval plan-
ning, shortcomings of various types of heavy
ordnance, irregularities in the award of ice
contracts, and militia brutality in the mas-
sacre of Indians at Sand Creek, Colorado.
These investigations brought to light
abuses which might otherwise have remained hidden, possibly to be repeated on
a larger scale.

Last but not least, as T. Harry Williams
has shown, the committee was a splendid
propaganda agency. Its investigations of
"rebel barbarities," first at Manassas and
then at Fort Pillow (to say nothing of its
revelations about the treatment of Union
soldiers in Southern prison camps), resulted in fiery pamphlets calculated to stir
the spirit of the North. The members excelled in this work, and there is little doubt
that their reports accomplished their purpose.

The committee's successes, then, seem
impressive. Operating under a rule of
secrecy, however, the members soon found
themselves accused of conducting an inquisition. Powerful generals were said to
tremble at the prospects of a confrontation
with "Bluff Ben" Wade and his colleagues.

That the body was really comparable to
a court of the star chamber is to be
doubted. Unquestionably, conservative
generals did not relish the prospect of in-
terrogation by their political opponents;
but, although without counsel, they certainly were neither cowed nor silenced by
the committee. George McClellan was the
investigators' principal target. Most of
them considered him a virtual traitor, but
he was given ample opportunity to testify.
In spite of intensive questioning, he di-

vulged no more than he wanted to reveal. When first summoned, he failed to appear altogether; when he finally testified several weeks later, he gave evasive answers and infuriated the members by his emphasis on the necessity of covering his routes of retreat. The committee was wholly unable to shake him.

Far from seeking to conciliate the committee, McClellan did not even extend to its chairman the ordinary courtesies due a United States Senator. When Wade, who had arrived on the Peninsula to make a personal inspection, sought shelter from a shower beneath the portico of a house, troops chased the visitor and his party away. "You must not hold me responsible, gentlemen," explained General Sumner, the local commander. "I am not the general-in-chief. I must enforce the order of my superior."

If McClellan defied the committee while still in command, he evidently did not change after he had been deposed. Testifying again in February and March, 1863, he set forth his views of the Peninsular campaign. Because he was fully aware of his questioners' hostility, he was nervous and paced the floor for seven minutes before replying, but he was again given a full hearing and refused to concede anything to the committee. His friends in Congress bitterly attacked the investigators, and the newspapers which supported him heaped abuse upon Wade, Chandler, the committee as a whole, and all its works.

What was true of McClellan was equally true of General William B. Franklin. Franklin was a conservative, generally in agreement with McClellan's views. That the committee would not be sympathetic must have been clear to him; nevertheless, when he testified on December 26, 1861, he steadfastly refused to divulge McClellan's plans. No matter how closely the investigators pressed him, he consistently defended his superior. One year later, the committee was to blame him for the disaster at Fredericksburg; the general, nothing daunted, published a scathing reply to his critics.

Quartermaster General Montgomery Meigs was another conservative who was far from overborne by the interrogators. In reply to questions as to why McClellan did not convoke frequent councils of his generals, Meigs stated that Napoleon had not relied on any such methods either. In answering queries about McClellan's projected movements, the Quartermaster General refused to commit himself on the ground that he did not know the commander's plans. No matter how intensely he was interrogated, he would not testify to the committee's satisfaction.

Other generals were equally uncooperative. Henry W. Slocum, when asked whether it would not be better to move at once, said that he could not answer any such question. Let the committee ask McClellan; *he* had the information! General George A. McCall, in answer to a similar query, replied that it would be preferable to move in the spring.

When, in 1864, the committee was reestablished with even greater powers, its procedure did not change very much. It continued its hearings and harassed its opponents, but did not habitually overawe them. General George G. Meade, one of its chief antagonists who was well aware of its reputed powers of doing harm, commented about the polite manner in which he was treated. And neither Grant nor Sherman, both of whom had at times felt the investigators' hostility, testified under any duress nor changed his actions in the least to accommodate the body.

If these officers did not necessarily feel they were confronting an inquisition, why did the committee have such a bad reputation? The reason was chiefly to be found in the strange case of General Charles P. Stone, the regular army officer who became the scapegoat for the disaster at Ball's Bluff, the occasion for the agency's establishment in the first place. Stone had been in command of the force under Colonel Edward Baker which was wiped out by the Confederates in October, 1861. Because of this circumstance, he was eventually blamed not merely for the defeat, but also for encouraging friendly relations with the enemy, returning fugitive slaves to their masters, and lack of sympathy for the Federal cause. His first appearance before the investigators was not particularly painful, but a number of his officers then gave testimony which was extremely damaging to him. His loyalty was impugned and the members of the committee began to consider him a traitor.

Late in January, 1862, the general made a second appearance before the committee. Confronted with serious charges affecting his competence and loyalty, he defended himself in a spirited manner. Since he was not given the opportunity to cross-examine witnesses, however, he found it difficult to contradict the accusations made against him. A few days later, he was arrested by order of the Secretary of War, lodged in prison in New York harbor, and held without trial for 189 days, not to be released until the passage of a law requiring speedy courts-martial.

Stone's misfortunes have often been blamed on the committee. It is undoubtedly true that the members were bitterly hostile to him and that they were misled by false charges which they turned over to the War Department; it is also true that they were deeply involved in Stone's downfall. It was Secretary Stanton, however, who ordered the general's arrest. As Wade pointed out in the Senate in reply to accusations of having introduced despotic

methods to America, Stone was arrested by the Lincoln administration—to be sure, after the committee had submitted testimony incriminating him. The general had been imprudent when he had sought to provoke Senator Sumner to a duel, and while there is no doubt that he was treated most unjustly, the committee itself finally gave him a fair hearing after his release. By that time it was more interested in blaming McClellan than his subordinates, so that eventually it wrote a comparatively moderate report about Stone. The affair, therefore, may be viewed as an exception rather than the rule.

Another miscarriage of justice has also sometimes been blamed on the committee. General Fitz-John Porter, one of McClellan's supporters and an outspoken critic of the Radicals, was court-martialed and dismissed from the service after Second Bull Run for alleged failure to support General Pope properly. But although he and certain of his subordinates had proven most uncooperative witnesses before the committee, the body did not play a direct role in his dismissal. Individual members encouraged Pope to take action against Porter, and the Radicals in general were looking for a scapegoat, but the charges were preferred by Pope at a time when the committee was not even in session.

The committee has also been attacked for its interference with Lincoln. Did it not harass the executive incessantly, demand ever more radical measures, and make Lincoln's exacting task even more difficult? Evidence for this point-of-view is again not overwhelming. While it is true that certain members were bitterly antagonistic to the President and that others criticized him frequently, as David Donald has shown, the rift between the Radicals and Lincoln was not as great as has sometimes been supposed. The principal investigators and the President both believed in the same fundamental objectives—the preservation of the Union and the need for emancipation—even though the chief executive did not take a stand for abolition as early as men like Wade and Chandler. In many ways he used the group, taking advantage of its impatience in a manner so skillful as to bring about great reforms despite conservative opposition.

A good example of this interaction may be found in the President's treatment of McClellan. That the general remained inactive for too long in 1861–1862 was as apparent to the President as to the committee, and he sought to utilize the investigators' pressure to goad the reluctant commander. When the group came to call on him at the White House on December 31, 1861, he received his visitors politely. What did the gentlemen have in mind, he asked. "Mr. President," stormed the chairman, "you are murdering your country by inches in consequence of the inactivity of the military and the want of a distinct policy in regard to slavery." According to reports which reached the diplomatic corps, the President said nothing in reply, but on the next day he wrote to McClellan, who had refused to commit himself. As Lincoln put it, he knew that the committee had been giving the general some uneasiness, but he assured McClellan that the gentlemen of the committee, who had been with him for an hour and a half the night before, were in a perfectly "good mood." They were beginning to see things much as "all sensible men would"—a gentle reminder that McClellan had better bestir himself.

Since the general did not take the hint, the President made further use of the pressures emanating from the committee. During the following weeks, the congressional investigators, continuing their harassment of the administration, urged incessantly that the "Young Napoleon" be shelved

and Irvin McDowell put in his place. Although it was a period of great difficulty for Lincoln—"the bottom is out of the tub," he complained to Montgomery Meigs—he knew how to make the most of the committee's impatience. On the advice of the Quartermaster General he called in McClellan's subordinates to confer about the general's failure to act. The commander heard about the conference, and, recovering quickly from a bout with typhoid fever, appeared in person to keep his enemies from dividing up "his military goods and chattels." Assuring the President that he had a good plan, he eventually unfolded a scheme to attack Richmond from the coast.

In the meantime, cooperation between the committee and the administration had become more effective. Because of his inefficiency, Secretary of War Cameron had been replaced by Edwin M. Stanton. The new Secretary, who saw eye-to-eye with the committee on many things, maintained a close relationship with its leading members. Hardly a day passed when he did not confer with them, and, although McClellan had originally considered him a friend, Stanton was scarcely less hostile to the general than the investigators. Under these circumstances, it was not surprising that Lincoln issued his General War Order No. 1, demanding an advance on February 22, 1862, and when it came to placing the armies in readiness, the Secretary of War sought congressional support through the chairman of the committee. Legislation requesting larger powers for the executive—wartime control of railroads and telegraph lines, for example—could always be initiated by the chairman, and unpopular acts, such as the imprisonment of General Stone, could be defended by him. The administration did not even feel particularly embarrassed by the committee's insistence that it move against slavery; the pressure exerted by the Radicals on one side could well be utilized to offset resistance by the conservatives on the other. And when the war spirit lagged, the committee could always perform a service by whipping up the nation's enthusiasm with its propaganda.

In spite of the President's order McClellan still refused to advance on February 22. Instead, well aware of the continual pressure from the committee, he explained his plans for the Peninsular campaign. Lincoln, whose faith in the general's strategy was not absolute, was not wholly convinced; he insisted that enough troops be left behind to protect Washington. Accordingly, he arranged a safeguard by dividing the Army of the Potomac into corps commanded by experienced officers who did not always agree with the Young Napoleon—a plan long advocated by the committee. Moreover, to provide, among other things, for the safety of the capital, he detached Blenker's division and later McDowell's corps, another one of the committee's pet schemes. Troublesome as the investigators were at times, they had their convenient aspects, even for Abraham Lincoln.

Finally, there remains the question of the committee's direct influence. An agency reputedly so sinister and dangerous would appear to have wielded much real power, but upon closer examination this proves hardly the case. In its effort to influence the conduct of the war the committee did strengthen Lincoln in his determination not to denude the defenses of Washington in the spring of 1862, it contributed materially to the changes brought about by the new corps organization, and it also succeeded in its primary objective of securing the removal of McClellan and his chief supporters. Moreover, by continuing its investigations of the Peninsular campaign after McClellan's dismissal, it

strengthened the hand of the administration in keeping the troublesome general in retirement. But these victories were not repeated in other fields. From beginning to end, Abraham Lincoln retained supreme authority; he permitted the committee to wield influence when it suited him to do so, but he turned a deaf ear when it did not.

The story of McClellan's dismissal—perhaps the committee's most important accomplishment—is the clearest example of this tendency. As early as December, 1861, Ben Wade and his colleagues demanded the sacking of the Young Napoleon. They stormed, they threatened, they begged; yet McClellan remained in command. "Put yourself in my place for a moment," said Lincoln to Wade on one occasion when he was being pressed for the general's dismissal. "If I relieve McClellan, whom shall I put in command?"

"Why, anybody!" replied the Senator.

"Wade," said Lincoln, "anybody will do for you, but not for me. I must have somebody." It was not until November, 1862, when the committee was not even in session, that Lincoln finally gave in. Fully realizing McClellan's faults himself, he dismissed him for good.

What was true of the committee's effort in respect to the McClellan dismissal was also true of its attempts to secure Benjamin F. Butler's return to New Orleans. The flamboyant ex-Democrat-turned-Radical had endeared himself to the group because of his shrewd characterization of fugitive slaves as "contraband of war"; he had testified that McClellan's estimates of enemy strength were grossly exaggerated; and when he was sent to New Orleans, he seemed to justify the committee's trust by ruling the city with an iron hand. Then, after having caused trouble for the State Department, he was recalled, his popularity, however, heightened by the fact that he had been declared an outlaw by Jefferson Davis. Arriving in Washington, he testified before the committee with great spirit, but he was unable to gain reappointment to the Crescent City. No matter how friendly the investigators were toward him, they simply did not have the power to help him.

The case of General John C. Fremont, too, illustrates that the committee's powers were limited. Delighted with the Pathfinder's vigorous action against slavery in Missouri in 1861, many Radicals had been furious about his dismissal even before the establishment of the investigating agency. When the committee was finally constituted, the members persisted in their efforts to have Fremont reinstated. Advertising his abilities, they pleaded with the administration to make amends. Although Lincoln finally assigned the general to the relatively unimportant Mountain Department, the Pathfinder was never satisfied with his new command. Unable to obtain a more important post, he bungled a campaign against Stonewall Jackson and eventually retired to New York, never to serve in the field again. Lincoln had taken his measure of Fremont in 1861. He was willing to give him a second chance in 1862, but when the officer failed to prove himself, neither the committee nor the general's other Radical friends could prevent his retirement.

General Ambrose Burnside also found that the influence of the committee was not as strong as he might have believed. After the disastrous defeat at Fredericksburg, Wade and his colleagues arrived at Falmouth to take testimony. What they heard fully restored their faith in the general who talked like a Radical. Interested in blaming his conservative subordinates for Burnside's misfortunes, the committee sought to refurbish his tarnished reputation by writing a favorable report about him

and generally lauding his good qualities. But when Burnside's own officers became unruly, he could not be saved, despite a further investigation after Joseph Hooker, another favorite of the committee, had taken his place. Lincoln refused to put up with him any longer.

The original Joint Committee on the Conduct of the War expired thirty days after the adjournment of the Thirty-seventh Congress on March 4, 1863, so that the investigating agency was not in existence when Lincoln removed Hooker and appointed George Meade to lead the Army of the Potomac. Parenthetically, it might be noted that, in spite of this handicap, the chairman and his friends made every effort to save Hooker after his defeat at Chancellorsville. They were no more successful than before. Lincoln was the commander-in-chief, and he was determined to exercise his prerogatives.

When the Thirty-eighth Congress met in December, 1863, it reconstituted the committee and gave it additional powers of subpoena and investigation. Nevertheless, what had been true of the former committee was also true of its theoretically stronger successor. It could investigate, it could make propaganda, it could seek to induce Lincoln to take radical measures, but it was the President who made the final decisions.

The most obvious indication of the committee's limited influence was the appointment of U. S. Grant as lieutenant general. Not that the members opposed the hero of Vicksburg—they had overcome their dislike for the Western commander long before—but neither the chairman nor any of the members were even consulted when the President made his decision. Since the appointment was one of the most important steps affecting the command structure taken during the war, the committee's relative impotence was evident. When the bill creating the new rank came up in the Senate, Wade himself, it is true, voted for an amendment which would have conferred the honor upon Grant by name; but the new commander was never beholden to the committee. He pursued his policies in the way he saw fit, and no group of politicians was able to interfere with him during the war.

Grant's retention of General Meade is a case in point. The commander of the Army of the Potomac had aroused the committee's displeasure for various reasons. Conservative in politics, he was believed to be an adherent of McClellan; cautious in battle, he was reputed to lack vigor. Did he not allow Lee to escape after the battle of Gettysburg? The indecisive Mine Run campaign in the fall of 1863 did nothing to change this estimate. In addition, General Daniel Sickles, one of the committee's favorites, had become Meade's bitter enemy and consistently testified against him. The result was that Wade and his colleagues repeatedly demanded Meade's dismissal. All their entreaties were in vain. The general remained in command.

What was true of Meade was equally true of Henry Wager Halleck, Lincoln's intellectual if somewhat inefficient Chief of Staff. Anathema to the members of the committee because of his West Point origins, his caution, and his traditionalism, the Chief of Staff could not be displaced. "Give Halleck 20,000 men and he couldn't raise three sitting geese," observed Ben Wade, but the general, for better or worse, remained in the capital transmitting orders.

During the last months of the President's life the committee's waning influence again became evident. When General Butler was summarily removed from command after his failure to take Fort Fisher, he embarked upon a vendetta against Grant. Sympathizing with the deposed commander, the members granted him an extensive hearing in which he convinced them of his innocence of any wrongdoing, but they found it impossible to overcome Grant's decision to drop the difficult Yankee. Butler had to return to his home at Lowell, never to serve on active duty again.

The accession of Andrew Johnson seemed to give the committee one last opportunity to gain influence. Having once been a member of the group, the new President was considered favorably inclined toward its views. "Johnson, we have faith in you. By the gods, there will be no trouble now in running the government," remarked the chairman when the committee called upon its former associate, who agreed that treason must be made infamous and traitors impoverished. The war was almost over, however, and Congress had adjourned. All that the committee could do was to call, for the last time, witnesses to bolster Radicals and discredit conservatives. Then it had to wind up its affairs, Congress having given it three months in which to do so. This it did with vigor, the members working with enthusiasm to prepare reports which constituted a monument to their industry and a great help to future historians.

If the committee's power was so circumscribed, why is it that it has been the subject of so much condemnation? The reason, it appears, is that the accomplishments of the congressional Radicals have often been ascribed solely to it and that, in spite of its limitations, it helped materially to strengthen the extremist cause. Interrogating hundreds of witnesses, it produced eight major volumes of testimony and a number of special reports—permanent records of its perseverance. Its merciless revelations about corruption, its forthright condemnation of malefactors, its powerful propaganda, and its ceaseless attacks upon conservative generals made it easier for Lincoln to bring about necessary changes. But it was only one of the means the Radicals employed to gain their ends, and since the President was quite willing to be pushed by them, albeit at his own speed, they were quite successful. It is therefore easy to confuse the achievements of all the Radicals with those of the committee.

In conclusion, then, it would appear that the Joint Committee on the Conduct of the War was something less than an inquisition. Operating within restrictions placed upon it by Congress, it could and did interrogate officials high and low, but lacked the power to dismiss or appoint them. It excelled in producing propaganda, served as Lincoln's goad, and became an important vehicle for the Radicals. Despite its errors, it performed a significant service. But the service was one of persuasion rather than action. It simply did not possess the power to act.

Illustrative of the quantitative method in identifying a political group is the statistical analysis of Radical representatives by GLENN M. LINDEN (b. 1928). Assistant professor of history at New Mexico State University, he wrote his doctoral dissertation at the University of Washington on "Congressmen 'Radicalism,' and Economic Issues, 1861–1873." His study is valuable both for its methods and its results. Observing that the older methods had produced disagreement, he sought greater precision. It is important to note how he endeavored to make a more exact analysis and what questions he set himself, as well as his conclusions.*

Glenn M. Linden

The Actual Vote
of Radical Representatives

In a recently published volume entitled *The Politics of Reconstruction,* Professor David Donald urges the use of new approaches to the persistent and complex problems of the reconstruction period. Recognizing the virtual exhaustion of conventional sources— newspapers, documents, manuscripts—he points the way toward a new methodology.

The present little book is intended to suggest an approach which may bypass these road blocks which have done so much to retard the rewriting of Reconstruction history. It consists of three exercises in applying techniques more frequently used in the behavioral sciences to the history of the Republican party during the years from 1863 to 1867, years during which this organization controlled the national government and set forth the conditions on which reunion could occur.

He proceeds to examine the voting records of individual Republican representatives in relation to the relative security or insecurity of their congressional seats. In this way he has sought to find a criterion for analyzing the groupings within the Republican party.

The need for a fresh approach to reconstruction is nowhere more obvious than in the continuing controversy among historians over "Radicals" and "Radicalism." In recent years increasing attention has been devoted to this area and yet no real agreement as to the identity of the Radicals or the nature and extent of their programs has been reached. This can be seen by examining the published views of four prominent Civil War and reconstruction historians—Howard K. Beale, T. Harry

*Glenn M. Linden, " 'Radicals' and Economic Policies: The House of Representatives, 1861–1873," *Civil War History,* XIII (March, 1967), 51–65. Some footnotes omitted.

Williams, David Donald, and Eric McKitrick.

Beale, in *The Critical Year: A Study of Andrew Johnson and Reconstruction* (1930), pictured a band of men with fanatical purposes, a minority of the Republican party determined to win their objectives whatever the cost. By the end of the war, "a few earnest men with fanatical perseverance had conquered a nation. With success the objectives broadened, but Thad Stevens and Ben Wade led the same movement in 1867 that Lovejoy and Garrison had served thirty years earlier."

Williams, in *Lincoln and the Radicals* (1941), wrote that the Radicals were the driving force in Congress during the Civil War years: "The radicals stood for instant emancipation, the confiscation of rebel property, the use of colored soldiers, civil and, when it should become expedient, political equality for the Negro," however little they cared for the Negro except as an instrument to fasten Republican political and economic control upon the South. By the end of the war, "They had conquered Lincoln, they would conquer Johnson."

Donald, in *Lincoln Reconsidered* (1956), questioned the validity of this view of the Radicals and stated that they ". . . were not united upon any positive social and economic program," but "they more nearly agreed about the things they opposed." Along with millions of other Americans they disliked slavery, fumbling military leadership, and Lincoln's slowness.

McKitrick's study, *Andrew Johnson and Reconstruction* (1960), also challenged the traditonal concept of "radicalism," arguing that as late as 1865, there was no " 'hard core' of plotters waiting to throw off the mask and take over the country." He carefully analyzed the meaning of "radicalism" and stated that the Radical legend was largely the result of Democratic efforts to brand the entire Republican party as fanatical and dominated by a hard core of Radical plotters.

It can readily be seen that there is substantial disagreement as to the unity and purpose of the Radicals in both the political and economic areas. Radicals are pictured as fanatical men seeking extreme ends, yet lacking a positive social or economic program. In order to offer a more precise analysis of this problem, the writer has examined the voting records of representatives in Congress from July, 1861 to March, 1873 (Thirty-seventh through the Forty-second Congresses); and by this quantitative method, has sought to identify the Radicals by name.

The first step in the identification of political Radicals during the years under consideration was the listing of representatives described as Radical by the authors of several standard histories of the reconstruction era. A more stringent test was the writer's examination of votes on various bills that from their substance may be considered Radical measures.

Thirty-four representatives (all Republicans) and twenty measures were identified as Radicals by the historians cited. To verify this identification of men and measures, the final vote on each bill was examined, and each representative classified as a supporter or opponent of Radical legislation. The results showed that all thirty-four Radical Republican representatives voted 75 per cent or more of the time in support of the Radical measures. However, most of the remaining Republican representatives voted for these same measures; the Democrats voted in a solid block against them. Only 8 per cent of the Republicans (23) and 4 per cent of the Democrats (6) failed to vote with their respective parties a majority of the time—of the 276 Republicans and 141 Democrats voting in the period from 1861 to 1873.

Table I†

Radical Representatives

Name	State	July 1861–April 1865	May 1865–Nov. 1866	Dec. 1866–March 1873
*Ashley, J. M.	Ohio	X (R)	X (R)	X (R)
Blaine, J. G.	Maine	X (R)	X	X (R)
Bingham, J. A.	Ohio	X (R)	X	X
Baker, J.	Ill.		X (R)	X
*Boutwell, G. S.	Mass.	X (R)	X (R)	X (R)
*Broomall, J.M.	Pa.	X (R)	X (R)	X (R)
*Butler, B. F.	Mass.			X (R)
*Covode, J.	Pa.	X (R)		X (R)
*Conkling, R.	N.Y.	X (R)	X (R)	
*Colfax, S.	Ind.	X (R)	X (R)	
Dawes, H. L.	Mass.	X (R)	X (R)	X
*Davis, H. W.	Md.	X (R)		
*Donnelly, I.	Minn.	X (R)	X (R)	X (R)
*Eliot, T. D.	Mass.	X (R)	X (R)	X (R)
Garfield, J. A.	Ohio	X (R)	X (R)	X
*Gooch, D. W.	Mass.	X (R)		
*Julian, G. W.	Ind.	X (R)	X (R)	X (R)
*Kelley, W. D.	Pa.	X (R)	X (R)	X (R)
Logan, J. A.	Ill.			X
*Lovejoy, O.	Ill.	X (R)		
Loan, B. F.	Mo.	X (R)	X (R)	X
Moorhead, J. K.	Pa.	X (R)	X (R)	X
*Morrill, S. P.	Maine			X (R)
*Nixon, J. T.	N.J.	X (R)		
*Pike, F. A.	Maine	X (R)	X (R)	X (R)
*Riddle, A. G.	Ohio	X (R)		
Schenck, R. C.	Ohio	X (R)	X (R)	X
*Sedgwick, C. B.	N.Y.	X (R)		
*Shellabarger, S.	Ohio	X (R)	X (R)	X (R)
Stevens, T.	Pa.	X	X (R)	X (R)
*Washburne, E. B.	Ill.	X (R)	X (R)	X (R)
*Wentworth, J.	Ill.		X (R)	
*Williams, W.	Ind.			X (R)
*Wilson, J. T.	Ohio			X (R)

†X indicates the period in which the representative was in office and voting and (R) indicates that he voted Radical in that period.

In order to identify the Radicals more precisely, amendments to the above measures, plus others considered appropriate by the writer, were examined. A total of seventy-six roll-call votes, ranging from the Confiscation Act of 1862 through the Resolutions on Arkansas and Louisiana in 1873, were collected,[1] and constitute the writer's test of Radicalism during the period from 1861 to 1873.

Of the thirty-four representatives named as Radical by historians, twenty-four met the more rigorous standard set by the author. Ten, including Thaddeus Stevens, failed to support Radical measures (1) in at least 75 per cent of the votes they cast on the seventy-six roll-call votes, and (2) for all the terms they served in the House of Representatives from 1861 to 1873.[2] These representatives are listed in Table I. The asterisk signifies those representatives who were considered Radical by both the historians and the author.

In examining the voting behavior of the Radicals, the author found 106 other representatives who were not mentioned by historians. These, together with twenty-four of the original thirty-four cited by historians, make a total of 130 representatives who supported Radical measures at least 75 per cent of the time they voted and in all the terms they served in Congress from 1861 to 1873. They are listed in Table II.

A list of "Non-Radical" representatives was also compiled—those who voted less than 50 per cent of the time in favor of Radical measures on the seventy-six roll-call votes during their terms in the House from 1861 through 1873. This Non-Radical list included the names of eighty-three representatives, shown in Table III.

Those representatives whose voting records were neither Radical nor Non-Radical (as defined above) were classified as "Non-Aligned."

With representatives identified as Radical, Non-Radical, or Non-Aligned, it is possible to examine economic policies and programs and determine possible political-economic relationships. The sharp division among historians over the nature and extent of Radical economic activity has centered around the degree of unity among Radicals and the type of program they sought to enact into law.

In order to provide quantitative evidence of possible political-economic relationships, the author collected sixty-five votes on economic measures, ranging from the Legal Tender Act of 1862 to the Salary Grab Act of 1873.[3] The previous classification of representatives as Radical, Non-Radical, and Non-Aligned was followed. The voting record of Radical representatives on roll-call votes on economic measures was examined and a "majority Radical vote" for each issue established. Then each representative's voting record was compared with the majority Radical vote and a percentage of agreement determined. Previously, 130 representatives

---

[1]The list of the test measures can be found in Glenn M. Linden, "Congressmen, 'Radicalism,' and Economic Issues 1861-1873." (Ph.D. dissertation, University of Washington, 1963), pp. 216–222. . . . A few of the key measures used were: Confiscation Act, Thirteenth Amendment, Wade Davis Bill, Freedmen's Bureau Bill, Civil Rights Bill, Fourteenth Amendment, Reconstruction Act over veto, Omnibus Bill, Fifteenth Amendment, Bill to Admit Virginia, Bill to Admit Georgia, Enforcement Act, Ku Klux Klan Act, Resolution to Count Louisiana Electoral Votes.

[2]Thaddeus Stevens of Pennsylvania supported the Radical position 63 per cent of the time during the Civil War, 100 per cent during moderate reconstruction, and 95 per cent during radical reconstruction.

[3]A list of the measures considered and the issues involved in the sixty-five roll-call votes may be found in Linden, "Congressmen, 'Radicalism,' and Economic Issues," pp. 254–255, 264, 270–273. Among the measures considered were the following: Legal Tender Act, Homestead Bill, National Currency Bill, Gold Bill, Loan Bill, Reduction of Currency Bill, Public Credit Bill, National Currency Bill, Salary Grab Act.

Table II
Radical Representatives (total list)

Name	State	July 1861– April 1865	May 1865– Nov. 1866	Dec. 1866– March 1873
Alley, J. B.	Mass.	X	X	X
Allison, W. B.	Iowa	X	X	X
Anderson, G. W.	Mo.		X	X
Anderson, L.	Ky.	X		
Ames, O.	Mass.	X	X	X
Arnold, I. N.	Ill.	X		
Ashley, J. M.	Ohio	X	X	X
Banks, N. P.	Mass.		X	X
Barker, A. A.	Pa.		X	
Baxter, P.	Vt.	X	X	
Beaman, F. C.	Mich.	X	X	X
Beatty, J.	Ohio			X
Benjamin, J. F.	Mo.		X	X
Boutwell, G. S.	Mass.	X	X	X
Brooks, G. M.	Mass.			X
Bromwell, H.P.H.	Ill.		X	X
Broomall, J. M.	Pa.	X	X	X
Buckland, R. P.	Ohio		X	X
Buffinton, J.	Mass.	X		X
Bundy, H. S.	Ohio		X	
Burdett, S. S.	Mo.			X
Butler, B. F.	Mass.			X
Churchill, J. C.	N.Y.			X
Clarke, F.	N.Y.	X		
Clarke, R. W.	Ohio		X	X
Clarke, S.	Kans.		X	X
Coburn, J.	Ind.			X
Cole, C.	Calif.	X		
Colfax, S.	Ind.	X	X	
Conger, O. D.	Mich.			X
Conkling, R.	N.Y.	X	X	
Cook, B. C.	Ill.		X	X
Covode, J.	Pa.	X	X	X
Creswell, J. A. J.	Md.	X		
Cullom, S. M.	Ill.		X	X
Darling, W. A.	N.Y.		X	
Davis, H. W.	Md.	X		
DeFrees, J. H.	Ind.		X	
Delano, C.	Ohio		X	
Deming, H. C.	Conn.	X	X	
Dixon, N. F.	R.I.	X	X	X
Donnelly, I.	Minn.	X	X	X
Driggs, J. F.	Mich.	X	X	X
Eckley, E. R.	Ohio	X	X	X

Table II *(cont.)*

Radical Representatives

Name	State	July 1861– April 1865	May 1865– Nov. 1866	Dec. 1866– March 1873
Eggleston, B.	Ohio		X	X
Eliot, T. D.	Mass.	X	X	X
Farquhar, J. H.	Ind.		X	
Fenton, R. E.	N.Y.	X		
Frank, A.	N.Y.	X		
Gooch, D. W.	Mass.	X		
Grinnell, J. B.	Iowa	X	X	
Harding, A. C.	Ill.		X	X
Hart, R.	N.Y.		X	
Hayes, R. B.	Ohio		X	
Henderson, J. H. D.	Ore.		X	
Higby, W.	Calif.	X	X	X
Hill, R.	Ind.		X	X
Hill, J.	N.J.			X
Holmes, S. T.	N.Y.		X	
Hooper, S.	Mass.	X	X	X
Hubbard, J. H.	Conn.	X	X	
Hubbard, A. W.	Iowa	X	X	
Hubbell, J. R.	Ohio		X	
Hubbard, D.	N.Y.		X	
Hulburd, C. T.	N.Y.	X	X	X
Judd, N. B.	Ill.			X
Julian, G. W.	Ind.	X	X	X
Kellogg, F. W.	Mich.	X		
Kelley, W. D.	Pa.	X	X	X
Kelsey, W. H.	N.Y.			X
Ketcham, J. H.	N.Y.		X	X
Lawrence, W.	Ohio		X	X
Littlejohn, D. C.	N.Y.	X		
Longyear, J. W.	Mich.	X	X	
Loughridge, W.	Iowa			X
Lovejoy, O.	Ill.	X		
Lynch, J.	Maine		X	X
McClurg, J. W.	Mo.	X	X	X
McIndoe, W. D.	Wis.	X	X	
McKee, S.	Ky.		X	X
McRuer, D. C.	Calif.		X	
Mercur, U.	Pa.		X	X
Miller, G. F.	Pa.		X	X
Miller, S. F.	N.Y.	X		
Moore, W.	N.J.			X
Morrell, D. J.	Pa.			X
Morrill, S. P.	Maine	X		X

Table II *(cont.)*

Radical Representatives

Name	State	July 1861– April 1865	May 1865– Nov. 1866	Dec. 1866– March 1873
Myers, A.	Pa.	X		
Myers, L.	Pa.	X	X	X
Newell, W. A.	N.J.		X	
Nixon, J. T.	N.J.	X		
Packard, J.	Ind.			X
Paine, H. E.	Wis.		X	X
Patterson, J. W.	N.H.	X	X	
Perham, S.	Maine	X	X	X
Peters, J. A.	Maine			X
Pike, F. A.	Maine	X	X	X
Plants, T. A.	Ohio		X	X
Poland, L. P.	Vt.			X
Price, H.	Iowa	X	X	X
Rice, A.	Mass.	X	X	
Rice, J.	Maine	X	X	
Riddle, A. G.	Ohio	X		
Rollins, E. H.	N.H.	X	X	
Sawyer, P.	Wis.		X	X
Sedgwick, C. B.	N.Y.	X		
Shannon, T. B.	Calif.	X		
Shellabarger, S.	Ohio	X	X	X
Smith, J. A.	Ohio			X
Smithers, N. B.	Del.	X		
Spaulding, O. L.	N.Y.	X		
Thayer, M. R.	Pa.	X	X	
Thomas, J. L., Jr.	Md.		X	
Trowbridge, R. E.	Mich.		X	X
Twitchell, G.	Mass.			X
Tyner, J. N.	Ind.			X
Upson, W. H.	Ohio			X
Van Aernam, H.	N.Y.		X	X
Ward, H.	N.Y.		X	X
Warner, S. L.	Conn.		X	
Washburne, C. B.	Wis.			X
Washburne, E.	Ill.	X	X	X
Washburne, W.	Mass.	X	X	X
Welker, M.	Ohio		X	X
Wentworth, J.	Ill.		X	
Wilder, A. C.	Kans.	X		
Williams, W.	Ind.			X
Wilson, J. T.	Ohio			X
Wilson, S. F.	Pa.		X	X
Windom, W.	Minn.	X	X	X

Table III
Non-Radical Representatives

Name	State	July 1861– April 1865	May 1865– Nov. 1866	Dec. 1866– March 1873
Adams, G. M.	Ky.			X
Allen, W. J.	Ill.	X		
Anacona, S. E.	Pa.	X	X	
Archer, S.	Md.			X
Bailey, J.	Pa.	X		
Beck, J. B.	Ky.			X
Bergen, T. G.	N.Y.		X	
Biggs, B. T.	Del.			X
Bird, J. T.	N.J.			X
Boyer, B. M.	Pa.		X	X
Brooks, J.	N.Y.	X		X
Brown, J. S.	Wis.	X		X
Burr, A. G.	Ill.			X
Chanler, J. W.	N.Y.	X		
Coffroth, A. H.	Pa.	X		
Cox, S. S.	Ohio	X		
Dawson, J. L.	Pa.	X	X	
Denison, C.	Pa.		X	
Eden, J. M.	Ill.	X		
Eldredge, C. A.	Wis.	X	X	X
Finck, W. E.	Ohio	X	X	
Getz, J. L.	Pa.			X
Glossbrenner, A. J.	Pa.		X	
Hall, W. A.	Mo.	X		
Harris, B. G.	Md.	X	X	
Herrick, A.	N.Y.	X		
Hogan, J.	Mo.		X	
Holman, W. S.	Ind.	X		X
Hubbell, E.	N.Y.		X	
Humphrey, J. M.	N.Y.		X	X
Johnson, P.	Pa.	X		
Kernan, F.	N.Y.	X		
Kerr, M. C.	Ind.		X	X
Knapp, R. C.	Ill.	X		
Knott, J. P.	Ky.			X
Latham, G. R.	W. Va.		X	
Law, J.	Ind.	X		
Lazear, J.	Pa.	X		
Leblond, F. C.	Ohio	X	X	
Long, A.	Ohio	X		
Mallory, R.	Ky.	X		
Marshall, S. S.	Ill.		X	X
McCormick, J. R.	Mo.			X

Table III *(cont.)*

Non-Radical Representatives

Name	State	July 1861– April 1865	May 1865– Nov. 1866	Dec. 1866– March 1873
McCullough, H.	Md.		X	
Morrison, J. L. D.	Ill.	X		
Niblack, W. E.	Ind.		X	X
Nicholson, J. A.	Del.		X	X
Noble, W. P.	Ohio	X		
Noell, J. W.	Mo.		X	
O'Dell, M. F.	N.Y.	X		
O'Neill, J.	Ohio	X		
Pendleton, G. H.	Ohio	X		
Potter, C. N.	N.Y.			X
Radford, W.	N.Y.	X		
Randall, W. H.	Ky.	X	X	
Randall, S.	Pa.	X	X	X
Raymond, H. J.	N.Y.		X	
Rice, J. M.	Ky.			X
Rogers, A. J.	N.J.		X	
Ross, L. W.	Ill.		X	
Rousseau, L. H.	Ky.		X	
Shanklin, G. S.	Ky.		X	
Sitgreaves, C.	N.J.		X	
Smith, G. C.	Ky.	X		
Smith, W. C.	Vt.		X	
Steele, J.	N.Y.	X		
Steele, W.	N.J.	X		
Stiles, J. D.	Pa.	X		
Stone, F.	Md.			X
Strouse, M.	Pa.	X	X	
Stuart, J. T.	Ill.	X		
Swann, T.	Md.			X
Taber, S.	N.Y.		X	
Taylor, Nelson	N.Y.		X	
Trimble, L.	Ky.		X	X
Wells, E.	Mo.			X
Whaley, K. V.	W. Va.	X		
White, C.	Ohio	X		
Winfield, C. H.	N.Y.	X	X	
Wood, B.	N.Y.			X
Woodward, G. W.	Pa.			X
Wright, E. R. V.	N.J.		X	
Yeaman, G. A.	Ky.	X		

were identified as political Radicals, based on their support of the Radical position on at least 75 per cent of the votes they cast and for all the terms they served in the House of Representatives from 1861 through 1873. Applying the same standard to the sixty-five roll-calls on economic issues, only twenty-one of the 310 Radical representatives voted in agreement with the majority Radical vote on at least 75 per cent of the roll-calls and for all the terms they served in the House of Representatives from 1861 through March, 1873.[4] A total of sixty representatives voted in accord with the majority Radical vote 75 per cent or more of the time in all their periods in office; six voted in more than one period.[5] Of the thirty-four representatives identified by historians as Radical, only seven voted with the majority Radical vote during the periods examined.[6] Thus, the evidence gained from 141 roll-call votes indicates that the Radical representatives who voted alike on political issues did not vote alike to any great degree on economic issues.

Since there was little evidence of an economic voting pattern along party lines, the author sought one along geographical lines. The same sixty-five votes were arranged according to the area represented.

On this basis, 229 representatives voted in agreement with the other representatives from their geographic section on at least 75 per cent of the votes they cast on economic issues as described above and for all the terms they served in the House of Representatives from 1861 to 1873. In the first period, from 1861 to 1865, sixty-two of 131 representatives voted 75 per cent or more of the time in agreement with members of their own geographic section; in the second period, from May, 1865, to November, 1866, seventy-three of 141 representatives; and in the third period, December, 1866, to March, 1873, ninety-four of 189 representatives had the same degree of voting unity. To these figures may be added twenty representatives in the first period, sixteen representatives in the second period, and thirty-seven in the third period who voted with the other representatives from their geographical section 67 per cent or more of the time. The total figures show approximately two-thirds of the representatives voted on economic issues in conjunction with their colleagues from the same geographical area. These representatives are listed in Table IV.

Additional information was gathered concerning the age, geographical section and previous political affiliation of all Radicals and Non-Radicals. The average Radical was forty-five years of age; had been a Whig in the earlier part of his life; and came from the New England, Mid-Atlantic, and Midwest areas. Few Radicals had ever been Democrats and few came from the border or western regions. The average Non-Radical was forty-three years of age, of uncertain political activity in the pre-Civil War period, and from the border, midwestern and Mid-Atlantic states. Few differences can be seen between the groups in terms of age, geographical section or previous political affiliation.

[4] The twenty-one representatives were Arnold of Illinois, Ashley of Ohio, Beaman of Michigan, Boutwell of Massachusetts, Brooks of Massachusetts, Clarke of Ohio, Davis of Maryland, Dixon of Rhode Island, Eckley of Ohio, Ferry of Michigan, Hart of New York, Holmes of New York, Hubbard of Connecticut, Hubbard of New York, Kellogg of Michigan, Longyear of Michigan, Rice of Maine, Smith of Ohio, Trowbridge of Michigan, Twitchell of Massachusetts, and Washburne of Wisconsin.

[5] A list of these names may be found in Linden, "Congressmen, 'Radicalism,' and Economic Issues," pp. 64–65.

[6] The seven representatives are Ashley of Ohio, Boutwell of Massachusetts, Colfax of Indiana, Davis of Maryland, Pike of Maine, Riddle of Maine, and Schenck of Ohio.

Table IV

Representatives Aligned Geographically on Economic Issues

	Classifi-cation	State	*July 1861– April 1865*	*May 1865– Nov. 1866*	*Dec. 1866– March 1873*
NEW ENGLAND STATES					
Republicans:					
Ames, O.	R	Mass.		X	X
Baldwin, J. D.		Mass.		X	X
Banks, N. P.	R	Mass.		X	X
Benton, J.		N.H.			X
Brooks, G. M.	R	Mass.			X
Delano, C.	R	Mass.	X		
Deming, H. C.	R	Conn.		X	
Dixon, N. F.	R	R.I.		X	X
Hoar, G. B.		Mass.			X
Hubbard, J. H.	R	Conn.		X	
Jenckes, T. A.		R.I.			X
Kellogg, S. W.		Conn.			X
Loomis, D.		Conn.	X		
Lynch, J.	R	Me.			X
Marston, G.		N.H.		X	
Morrill, J. S.		Vt.		X	
Perham, S.	R	Me.		X	X
Rice, A. H.	R	Mass.	X	X	
Rollins, E. H.	R	N.H.	X	X	
Smith, W. C.	NR	Vt.			X
Starkweather, H. H.		Conn.			X
Twitchell, G.	R	Mass.			X
Woodbridge, F. E.		Vt.		X	X
MID-ATLANTIC STATES					
Republicans:					
Baker, S.		N.Y.	X		
Barker, A. A.	R	Pa.		X	
Blair, S. S.		Pa.	X		
Broomall, J. M.	R	Pa.			X
Chamberlain, J. P.		N.Y.	X		
Churchill, J. C.	R	N.Y.			X
Clarke, F.	R	N.Y.	X		
Covode, J.	R	Pa.	X		X
Darling, W. A.	R	N.Y.		X	
Donnelly, I.	R	Minn.			X
Duell, R. H.		N.Y.	X		
Fenton, R. E.	R	N.Y.	X		
Ferris, O.		N.Y.			X
Hale, R. S.		N.Y.		X	
Halsey, G. A.		N.Y.			X
Hickman, J.		Pa.	X		

Table IV *(cont.)*

Representatives Aligned Geographically on Economic Issues

Name	Classifi-cation	State	*July 1861–April 1865*	*May 1865–Nov. 1866*	*Dec. 1866–March 1873*
Hotchkiss, G. W.		N.Y.			X
Ketcham, J. H.	R	N.Y.		X	X
Lansing, W. E.		N.Y.	X		
Lawrence, G. V.		Pa.		X	X
Marvin, J. M.		N.Y.		X	X
McPherson, E.		Pa.	X		
Morrell, D. J.	R	Pa.			X
Olin, A. B.		N.Y.	X		
Packer, J. B.		Pa.			X
Scotfield, G. W.		Pa.		X	X
Sherman, S. N.		N.Y.	X		
Spaulding, E. G.	R	N.Y.	X		
Stewart, T. E.		N.Y.			X
Thayer, M. R.	R	Pa.		X	
Van Horn, B.		N.Y.	X	X	X
Van Valkenburgh, R. B.		N.Y.	X		
Verree, J. P.		Pa.	X		
Ward, H.	R	N.Y.		X	X
Wheeler, W. A.		N.Y.	X		X

Democrats:

Name	Classifi-cation	State	*July 1861–April 1865*	*May 1865–Nov. 1866*	*Dec. 1866–March 1873*
Bailey, J.	NR	Pa.	X		
Coffroth, A. H.	NR	Pa.		X	
Dawson, J. L.	NR	Pa.		X	
Haight, E.		N.Y.	X		
Steele, J. B.	NR	N.Y.	X		
Townsend, W.		Pa.			X
Winfield, C. H.	NR	N.Y.		X	

MIDDLE WESTERN STATES:

Republicans:

Name	Classifi-cation	State	*July 1861–April 1865*	*May 1865–Nov. 1866*	*Dec. 1866–March 1873*
Aldrich, C.		Minn.	X		
Ambler, J. A.		Ohio			X
Arnold, I. N.	R	Ill.	X		
Baker, J.		Ill.		X	X
Beaman, F. C.	R	Mich.	X	X	X
Blake, H. G. O.		Ohio	X		
Bromwell, H. P. H.		Ill.		X	
Cary, S. F.		Ohio			X
Clarke, R. W.	R	Ohio		X	X
Clarke, S.	R	Kans.			X
Cobb, A.		Wis.		X	X
Coburn, J.	R	Ind.			X
Colfax, S.		Ind.	X		

Table IV *(cont.)*

Representatives Aligned Geographically on Economic Issues

Name	Classifi- cation	State	July 1861– April 1865	May 1865– Nov. 1866	Dec. 1866– March 1873
Cook, B. C.	R	Ill.		X	X
Dunn, W. M.		Ind.	X		
Eckley, E. R.	R	Ohio			
Edgerton, S.		Ohio	X		
Farquhar, J. H.	R	Ind.		X	
Gurley, J. A.		Ohio	X		
Harding, A. C.	R	Ill.		X	
Hawley, J. B.		Ill.			X
Hopkins, B. F.		Wis.			X
Hutchins, J.		Ohio	X		
Judd, N. B.	R	Ill.			X
Kellogg, F. W.	R	Mich.	X		
Kellogg, W.		Ill.	X		
Lawrence, W.	R	Iowa		X	X
Logan, J. A.		Ill.			X
Loughridge, W.	R	Iowa			X
McCrary, G. W.		Iowa			X
Riddle, A. G.	R	Ohio	X		
Stillwell, T. N.		Ind.		X	
Trimble, C. A.		Ohio	X		
Tyner, J. N.	R	Ind.			X
Washburne, H. D.		Ind.			X
Williams, T.		Pa.		X	
White, A. S.		Ind.	X		
Worcestor, S. T.		Ohio	X		
Democrats:					
Eldredge, C. A.	NR	Wis.		X	
Granger, B. F.		Mich.	X		
Lehman, W. E.		Ohio	X		
Potter, C. N.	NR	Wis.	X		

Border States

Republicans:

Name	Classifi- cation	State	July 1861– April 1865	May 1865– Nov. 1866	Dec. 1866– March 1873
Anderson, G. W.	R	Mo.			X
Finkelnburg, G. A.		Mo.			X
Gravely, J. J.		Mo.			X
Latham, G. R.	NR	W. Va.		X	
Newcomb, C. A.		Mo.			X
Noell, J. W.	NR	Mo.		X	
Norton, E. H.		Mo.	X		
Polsley, D. H.		W. Va.			X
Van Horn, R. T.		Mo.		X	X
Webster, E. H.		Md.	X		

Table IV *(cont.)*

Representatives Aligned Geographically on Economic Issues

Name	Classifi-cation	State	July 1861–April 1865	May 1865–Nov. 1866	Dec. 1866–March 1873
Democrats:					
Adams, G. M.	NR	Ky.			X
Archer, S.	NR	Md.			X
Beck, J. B.	NR	Ky.			X
Biggs, B. T.	NR	Del.			X
Crittenden, J. J.		Ky.	X		
Dunlap, G. W.		Ky.	X		
Golladay, J. S.		Ky.			X
Grider, H.		Ky.		X	
Grover, A. P.		Ky.			X
Harding, A.		Ky.		X	
Hogan, J.	NR	Mo.		X	
Knott, J. P.	NR	Ky.			X
Mallory, R.	NR	Ky.	X		
McCormick, J. R.	NR	Mo.			X
Phelps, C. E.		Md.		X	
Stone, F.	NR	Md.			X
Trimble, L. S.	NR	Ky.		X	
Wells, E.	NR	Mo.			X

Other Parties

Conservative:

Ritter, B. C.		Ky.		X	

Unionist:

Wadsworth, W. H.		Ky.	X		

Pacific Coast

Republicans:

Ashley, D. R.		Nev.			X
McRuer, D. C.	R	Calif.		X	
Phelps, T. G.		Calif.	X		
Sargent, A. A.		Calif.	X		X

Democrats:

Axtell, S. B.		Calif.			X

Unionist:

Bidwell, J.		Calif.		X	

A number of conclusions can be drawn
om an examination of 141 roll-call votes
d the individual voting patterns of each
presentative:

1. 130 representatives have been identi-
d as Radical and eighty-three represen-
tives as Non-Radical in the period from
ly, 1861, to March, 1873. Their voting
cords on seventy-six roll-call votes sug-
sted a definite division along party lines
 political measures pertaining to the re-
nstruction of the southern states and
atment of the Negro.

2. Radical representatives, as defined
ove, did not maintain party unity on
ty-five roll-call votes on selected econom-
 issues. A similar lack of unity was ap-
rent among Non-Radicals. Rather, a
ossing of party lines on economic voting
d occur, with representatives from the
me geographical section voting together
respective of party affiliation.

3. Many Radical representatives did
t vote with representatives of their own
ographical area. For example, Hooper of
assachusetts voted with the majority of

his geographical section 58 per cent of the
time in the first period, 86 per cent in the
second period, and 73 per cent in the third
period. Also, Baxter of Vermont voted
with the majority of his geographical section 65 per cent in the first period and 100
per cent in the second period. Similarly,
many Non-Radicals and Non-Aligned representatives voted in the same manner.

Thus, the votes cast in the House of
Representatives from 1861 to 1873 constitute evidence supporting the description of
Radicals by Donald and McKitrick and
contrary to the views of Beale and Williams. It would appear that the Radicals
did not pursue clear-cut economic policies
and that there was little correlation between their economic and political voting
behavior. Economic voting patterns followed geographical, not political party
lines. It seems clear that traditional views
of Radicals and Radicalism need closer examination and the analysis of voting records offers one way of approaching this
problem.

In his sophisticated essay on the United States Senate,
ALLAN G. BOGUE (b. 1921), professor of history at the
University of Wisconsin, examines 368 roll calls to
ascertain the role of party, geography, and faction in
explaining Republican senators' votes during the fruitful
second session of the Thirty-seventh Congress. This work
differs from Linden's study of the House in important
respects. It restricts its analysis to a single session of the
wartime Senate. Moreover, it employs more advanced
quantitative techniques to determine voting behavior. A
significant aspect is Bogue's explanation and
exemplification of new research methods.*

Allan G. Bogue

The Actual Vote of Radical Senators

As he fought for election in 1854, James
Harlan explained how he would conduct
himself if elected to the Senate of the
United States: "... in all *Constitutional*
questions ... I would expect to be guided
in my action by the decisions of the
Supreme Court and the well-settled principles of Constitutional Law—in all questions of *Legislative Expediency,* by the views
and wishes of the Legislature and people of
Iowa—and in all questions of *Conscience* by
the Bible." To understand court, constituency and holy writ was to understand
the legislative behavior of Senator Harlan,
or so he said. The fact is that it is rather
difficult to understand Senator Harlan at
times in these terms or by any other simple
formula and this is also true of his col-

leagues in the Senate. Led, some time ag
to the Thirty-seventh or first Civil W.
Congress by my interest in the great ec
nomic legislation of that body, I soc
found myself trying to understand the m
jor forces that were reflected in the votir
of the congressmen. This paper is an ou
growth of that rather frustrating endea
or—a case study of general voting behavi
in the Senate during the second se
sion, the longest and most important of th
three legislative sessions of the Thirt
seventh Congress.

The historian who seeks for understanc
ing can, of course, usually find othe
historians willing to guide him. We are a
familiar with the interpretation which pi
tures a beleaguered Lincoln, strugglin

---

*Allan G. Bogue, "Bloc and Party in the United States Senate: 1861–1863. *"Civil War History,* XIII (Se
tember, 1967), 221–241. Some footnotes omitted.

uring the Civil War to maintain his lead-
rship against the determined onslaughts
f the Radical faction that dominated his
arty and the Congress. This organization-
l theme has been rewarding and, in-
eed, the authors of some of the historical
lassics of the Civil War have used it. But
cently David Donald has argued that
istorians have overstressed the difference
etween Radical and Moderate Republi-
ans and suggested that the importance of
arty bonds should be emphasized instead.
'. Harry Williams, however, continues to
elieve that the distinction is an important
ne. If we exclude the executive branch
om our discussion and focus on the con-
ressional aspects of the Radical-Moderate
ontroversy it is clear that the problem can
e stated more precisely. Did party or did
actional groups within the Republican
arty more significantly influence the
oting of Republican senators and repre-
ntatives during the Civil War years?
More recently still, Professor Donald has
uggested that the congressional district
layed a major part in determining the
otes of members of the House of Repre-
ntatives when they were considering re-
onstruction legislation. Thus in a sense he
ined Senator Harlan in emphasizing the
nportance of constituency in helping to
etermine congressional voting patterns—
factor which may have accounted for the
resence of Moderate and Radical factions
mong the Republicans, if indeed they did
xist.

We remember also that Frederick Jack-
on Turner had something to say about the
elation of constituency to legislative be-
avior. "A study of votes in the federal
Iouse and Senate from the beginning of
ur national history reveals the fact,"
rote Turner, "that party voting has more
ften broken down than maintained itself
n fundamental issues; that when these

votes are mapped or tabulated . . . a persistent sectional pattern emerges." The
Thirty-seventh was of course the first congress of the Civil War and unusual in that
most of the representatives of one great
section were missing. Although the empty
seats render this and the next congress
unique in the history of national legislative
behavior, Earle Ross and others have
maintained that sectionalism, particularly
that of East against West, continued to influence the actions of legislators during the
Civil War. In the *Congressional Globe* we can
easily find proud affirmations of loyalty to
constituency, frank declarations of sectional interest, and the appeals of Republican
leaders to their colleagues to shun factionalism and cleave to party. But oratorical
flourishes can be deceiving; in the end it
was the votes of the senators that counted.
And what do the votes tell us of geographical bloc, of party faction and of the bonds
of party?

When I began this research I selected
for analysis all of the substantive votes
which were concerned with slavery and
confiscation measures, both broadly defined; the tariff and the internal revenue
tax bills; legal tenders; the agricultural
college bill; the homestead law; the department of agriculture bill; the Pacific
railroad act; northern civil liberties and
the general conduct of the war, as well as a
few important procedural votes that
seemed related to such measures. Most of
these votes fell into one of three broad categories. Eighty-seven dealt with the confiscation of rebel property or the status of
slavery; fifty-one emerged from the debate
on the Internal Revenue Act of 1862; and
the debates on other major economic legislation of national interest produced thirty-
five votes. During the course of the research I broadened the scope of the study
to include 368 roll calls of this session, ex-

cluding only those that related to appointments.[1] These votes are the major source
for the scholar seeking evidence of patterns
in the voting of the thirty-one Republicans, eleven Democrats, five Border Unionists and one Northern Unionist who sat
in the Senate during most of the second
session of the Thirty-seventh Congress.[2]

In the following pages I have used a few
simple devices that describe legislative behavior in quantitative terms.[3] An index
number of cohesion shows the extent to
which a political party or group is united
in a particular roll call on a scale running
from one to one hundred. Similarly, an index number of agreement or likeness measures the degree to which the members of
two parties or groups vote alike in a division, and the obverse of such a number can
be called an index of disagreement. Thus,
if Democrats and Republicans agreed on a
particular vote to the amount of 40 per
cent of the maximum agreement which
would result when all Republicans and all
Democrats voted alike, the index of likeness would be forty and the index of disagreement would be sixty.

Other techniques help us to identify

groups of legislators that act in concert, c
relative differences in attitude among legis
lators. If we record the number of time
that each legislator votes with every othe
legislator we can find groups of like
minded individuals by fitting the pai▸
agreement scores into a matrix with th▸
highest agreements in the upper left co▸
ner. Legislative groups derived by this pro
cess are often called cluster blocs. Th▸
Guttman scale deals with associatio▸
among the senators in a different way. I▸
effect, this variety of scaling procedure iso
lates a roll call in which a small group ▪
legislators vote against the rest of th▸
chamber and then adds to this roll ca.
others in which the members of the sma▸
group are in agreement but are joined, ro▸
call by roll call, by other legislators wh▸
vote with the original minority on subse
quent votes added. Because they coul▸
find few who shared their opinion on th▸
original roll call the members of the initia
small group are assumed to have held a▸
extreme or radical position on a particula▸
subject. The added roll calls express in
creasingly moderate views on the same are
of legislation until the last roll call adde
may perhaps contain only a small group i
opposition to the original minority—
group whose members are utterly oppose▪
to any legislative concession whatsoever o▪
the subject at issue. Roll calls arranged i▪
this way, therefore, form a scale whic▪
ranks congressmen according to their att▸
tude on legislative proposals dealing with
particular problem.

The cluster bloc technique may not re
veal the shifting patterns of agreemen▸
among legislators over time and gives n▪
hint of the relative extremeness in attitud
of group members in comparison with th▪
positions taken by the members of othe
groups. It may require the researcher t
make arbitrary decisions concerning th

---

[1] This included votes in the Senate proper, in committee of the whole and in executive session. Tallies
used are those recorded in the Senate *Journals*, supple-
mented occasionally by those in the *Congressional
Globe.*

[2] In the Border Unionist category I included five
senators of Whig origins from the Border States. I
have used the term Northern Unionist to describe
Senator Joseph A. Wright of Indiana. A prominent
Democrat prior to the Civil War, Wright was selected
by Governor Morton to replace Senator Bright and
abjured party politics for the duration of the war.

[3] An index of cohesion may be calculated by sub-
tracting the per cent yea of a party's vote (if the smaller) from the per cent nay (if the larger) or vice versa.
When 83 per cent of Republicans voted yea and 17
per cent voted nay on a bill the index number of
cohesion is $83-17=66$. If 75 per cent of the Democrats and 50 per cent of the Republicans voted yea
in a roll call the index of likeness or agreement is
$100-(75-50)=75$.

outer limits of the groups or clusters. The scalogram masks but does not completely destroy temporal relationships, does not isolate the members of self-conscious groups, and discards roll calls that will not scale. There also is involved in scaling the assumption that legislators will vote for measures which in their minds represent only half a loaf because half is, after all, better than none. Not all representatives and senators are so logical; some, in frustration, vote against bills because they deem them too weak and there are instances of such behavior in the Thirty-seventh Congress. But in general the principle holds. Indeed, John Sherman stated it neatly on one occasion in this Congress, "It is always better, in a legislative body ... to do the best you can. It is a principle by which I have always been governed. . . ." Neither the index number approach, the cluster bloc technique, nor the Guttman scale is perfect or all revealing but used together these methods can reveal a great deal about legislative behavior.

We should, of course, avoid imposing unreasonable standards in evaluating the behaviour of political groups or individual legislators. To expect voting blocs or factions to maintain the same membership over long periods of time is unrealistic. Wayne Morse, no matter what he would like to think, is hardly a unique creation of this harried age. It is similarly unrealistic to suppose that all legislators will maintain exactly the same ideological position over a period of two or more sessions, or even during one session. It is unreasonable to assume that group feeling must be reflected by agreement across a number of different kinds of issues or that all members of a group should reflect the same intensity of attitude concerning even those issues on which they most strongly agree.

The crucial defection or the betrayal of friends provides us with the high drama of political history but such acts must be viewed in the general perspective of voting frequencies and it is with these that we are mainly concerned here.

"We" [of the Northwest], said Senator Grimes, "are the only portion of all the loyal States that feel the effect of this war oppressively. . . . Whilst men who own the railroads in the Northwest are making fortunes out of this war by the transportation of our produce, we are receiving nothing in fact from it." Later in the session, Ten Eyck of New Jersey spoke for the East when he asked: "Now what inducement is there for a Senator from an Atlantic State to vote an appropriation of large sums of money, even in the shape of a loan, to construct a variety of [rail] roads for the advantage of the western States?" These were the oratorical flourishes of eastern and western sectionalism. We can quite easily design a procedure that will reveal the presence of sectional determinants in voting divisions.

In examining the roll calls of the Senate, I assumed that a disagreement index of forty or more represented substantial disagreement between eastern and western Republicans. Western Republican senators included all of those from Ohio or states to the west and eastern Republicans, those members of the party from the states east of Ohio. The states represented by Democrats were few and widely spread; I did not, therefore, use Democratic votes in my search for roll calls that revealed the sectionalism of east and west. By these definitions there was substantial sectional disagreement among eastern and western Republican senators in forty-six of the 368 votes of the second session.

The sectionalism of East and West appeared most frequently in voting on economic measures of national significance.[4] In the original selection of eighty-seven roll calls relating to slavery and confiscation and eighty-six that were linked to major economic legislation only 7 per cent of the slavery and confiscation roll calls showed substantial sectional disagreement between the eastern and western Republicans, in comparison to 25 per cent of the votes on economic policy. Consideration of all 368 roll calls does not change the generalization. In voting on slavery and confiscation measures, the Republican senators divided on the basis of East and West in seven substantive votes and in three procedural votes. The same pattern appeared in two roll calls concerning the possibility of expelling Lazarus Powell, senator from Kentucky. Among the votes on economic legislation we find a division between eastern and western Republicans on eight roll calls during the debates on the internal revenue bill; on eight votes in the discussion of the land grant college bill; on three concerning greenback issues; on three during the Pacific railroad debates; and two divisions concerning the tariff. Sectionalism appeared also in three votes relating to the judiciary, three concerning appropriations for the armed forces, and in five roll calls on miscellaneous matters.

Western Republicans ranged themselves against the eastern members of their party most sharply when they voted on the land grant college bill. Eight of the nine roll calls, generated in discussion of this bill, showed substantial disagreement between East and West; the index of disagreement between the sections ranged from seventy-one to eighty-five in the roll calls on the

major amendments. In the end both Wisconsin senators and one Republican senator from Iowa, Indiana, and Kansas actually voted against the bill. They were joined by Senator Wright, the northern Unionist from Indiana, whose Republican colleague supported the most severe amendments proposed by the westerners but did not vote on the bill itself. No other economic measure inspired such consistent and strong antagonism between eastern and western Republicans in this session.

Indices of likeness or disagreement do not reveal whether the representatives of a section were more united in their approach to certain categories of legislation than were the legislators of another section. But this was indeed the case among the Republican senators of the Thirty-seventh Congress. The average voting agreement among all possible pairs of western senators was 61 per cent (with absences deleted) in the roll calls on the major national economic legislation and 59 per cent in the votes on the internal revenue bill.[5] In contrast, the eastern Republicans had mean agreements of 76 and 65 per cent. The differences between the two groups of senators would have increased still more had I dropped the senators from the Middle States from the comparison. Six New England senators, Clark (N.H.), Collamer (Vt.), Fessenden (Me.), Foot (Vt.), Foster (Conn.), and Morrill (Me.) were in particularly strong agreement in the votes on economic legislation. Minimal mean agreement among these men was 73 per cent and Clark and Fessenden voted together in 97 per cent of the roll calls on major economic legislation. There was no western group comparable either in numbers or in the strength of agreement among its members.

---

[4] Of course, much of the legislation, passed or proposed, concerning the South was "economic" in both its short-run and long-run implications, but for the sake of convenience I will distinguish between legislation on slavery and confiscation (or southern legislation) in contrast to national economic legislation.

[5] Absences of individual senators are disregarded in the calculation of these percentages.

Among the 368 roll calls of the second session there were ninety-one in which the cohesion indices of eastern and western Republicans differed by as much as forty points. In fifty-nine of these roll calls it was the easterners who showed the greater solidarity. The western Republicans were more cohesive in voting on only thirty-two roll calls of this type. Of the 105 votes in this session which were apparently related to economic measures of national interest, thirty-five, or 33 per cent, showed a marked difference in the cohesion of eastern and western Republicans. Of 120 roll calls linked to slavery, confiscation and the general conduct of the war, only eighteen, or 15 per cent, revealed a similar pattern. Thus, economic issues provoked more sectional response between eastern and western Republicans than did legislation concerned with slavery and confiscation, and it is clear also that the eastern Republicans were in greater agreement on the national economic legislation of this Congress than were their western colleagues.

The most striking sectional alignment in Congress during the years before the Civil War had reflected the divergent interests of North and South. During most of the second session of the Thirty-seventh Congress senators represented five slave states. This group, containing both Democrats and former Whigs, guarded the southern heritage insofar as they considered it appropriate and feasible—which was sometimes a good deal further than the Republicans liked. An index of disagreement which compares the voting of the senators from the slave states with that of the senators from the free states shows substantial disagreement on 154 of the 368 Senate roll calls of this session. Sixty-seven of these votes appeared in the original selection of eighty-seven roll calls, related to slavery and confiscation legislation. The slave-state delegation was so small that this

bloc's voting was sometimes masked by other voting determinants, but the group could be of major importance when Radical and Moderate Republicans disagreed.

To examine the conflict of Radical and Moderate Republicans is more difficult than it is to examine sectional manifestations in Congress, as we have no ready-made categories to use. But the documentary evidence suggests that the distinction had real meaning among the legislators. In December, 1861, Timothy Howe of Wisconsin predicted factional strife in the party when he wrote:

Everything about us portends the coming of a rupture in the ranks of the war party and if so, a fierce struggle between the two factions. The organization of a party designing either to rule the administration or to supplant it has I think already commenced. Emancipation: the utter extinction of slavery will be the watchword & the effort of one faction. Where the other faction will plant itself is not so certain.

And if one reads only the debates on the confiscation bills of the next spring one finds the senators describing, explicitly or implicitly, the differences among Republicans. Some opponents of a harsh confiscation bill invoked the Constitution against those who maintained that Congress should exercise war powers and advocated "legislative encroachment upon the prerogatives of the other departments." But men who complained in this fashion, retorted Senator Wade, were contending for "the irresponsible power of the Chief Magistrate in time of war," a doctrine which he characterized as "most slavish and un-American." Senator Dixon, who feared that the powers of the states might be diminished, maintained that the rebel states were still within the Union and their residents, therefore, were entitled to the guarantees of the Constitution if they were to be punished. He also implied that the chairman of the Judiciary Committee was

Table I

A Voting Pattern on Slavery and Confiscation Measures

Senator	Party	State	Type	N 1	N 2	N 3	Y 4	N 5	N 6	Y 1	Y 2	Y 3	N 4	Y 5	Y 6
Powell	D	Ky.	6	*	*	*	*	*	*						
Kennedy	BU	Md.	6	*	*	*	0	*	0						
Davis	BU	Ky.	6	*	*	*	*	0	*						
Wilson, R.	BU	Mo.	6	*	*	0	*	*	.*						
Carlile	BU	Va.	6	*	*	*	0	*	*						
Wright	NU	Ind.	6	*	—	*	*	*	*		x				
Saulsbury	D	Del.	5		*	0	0	*	*	0					
Stark	D	Ore.	5		*	0	0	*	*	0					
Willey	BU	Va.	5		*	*	*	*	*	0					
Henderson	D	Mo.	4			*	*	*	*	*	*				
Cowan	R	Pa.	4			*	*	0	*	*	*				
Browning	R	Ill.	4			*	*	*	*	*	*				
Anthony	R	R.I.	3				*	*	*	*	*	*			
Doolittle	R	Wis.	3				*	*	*	*	*	*			
Collamer	R	Vt.	3				*	*	0	*	0	*			
Sherman	R	Ohio	3				*	*	*	*	*	*			
Foster	R	Conn.	3				*	*	*	*	*	*			
Ten Eyck	R	N.J.	3				*	*	*	*	*	*			
Fessenden	R	Me.	3				*	0	*	*	*	*			
Lane, H. S.	R	Ind.	3				*	*	*	0	*	0			
Simmons	R	R.I.	3				*	*	*	*	*	*			
Howe	R	Wis.	3				*	*	*	*	*	*			
Harris	R	N.Y.	2					*	0	*	*	*	*		
Foot	R	Vt.	2					*	*	*	*	*	*		
Clark	R	N.H.	1						*	*	*	*	*	*	*
Hale	R	N.H.	1						*	*	*	*	*	0	0
Wilson, H.	R	Mass.	1						*	*	*	*	*	*	*
Sumner	R	Mass.	1						*	*	*	*	*	*	*

an "opponent of this Administration." To this the chairman, Lyman Trumbull, responded by suggesting that Dixon was a "courtier" and a "sycophant" who did "not mean to be in opposition to the Administration let what will happen. ..." In this exchange we find support of the administration used to distinguish one Republican from another.

Senator Cowan referred to "the ultra school of the Republican party," whose members had decided that the rebellion of "some of the slave States" should be "put down by main force, and by an utter disregard of the will of the whole people of the slave States," and were insisting on measures "utterly obnoxious and distasteful" to every senator from the slave states. More personally still, Wade described himself and his friends as "the earnest, up and down, through thick and thin Republicans of this body," leaving the character of recusant Republicans to the imagination. But on one occasion, Fessenden, in exasperation with Wade and his friends, spoke of "certain gentlemen on this floor," who "seem to think that they are the representatives of all righteousness ... and that if anybody differs from them he is either a fool or a knave."

Table I *(cont.)*

A Voting Pattern on Slavery and Confiscation Measures

Senator	Party	State	Type	N 1	N 2	N 3	Y 4	N 5	N 6	Y 1	Y 2	Y 3	N 4	Y 5	Y 6
Morrill	R	Me.	1						*	*	*	*	*	0	
Lane, J. H.	R	Kan.	0					*		*	*	*	*	*	
Harlan	R	Ia.	0							*	*	*	*	0	0
Pomeroy	R	Kan.	0							0	*	0	*	*	*
Grimes	R	Ia.	0							*	0	*	*	*	*
Chandler	R	Mich.	0							*	*	*	*	*	*
Wilkinson	R	Minn.	0							*	*	*	*	*	*
Trumbull	R	Ill.	0							*	0	*	*	*	*
King	R	N.Y.	0							*	*	*	*	*	*
Wade	R	Ohio	0					x		*	*	*	*	—	*
Wilmot	R	Penn.	0							*	0	*	*	*	0

* = pattern vote; —x = deviant vote (error); 0 = absent. Forty-six other roll calls from the original selection fitted into this scale. Missing senators voted in less than half of the divisions shown here. Coefficient of reproducibility = .99.

Voting Key: 1—Final vote on S. 351, supplementary to the act for emancipation in the District of Columbia.

2—Final vote on S. 394, to amend the act calling forth the militia.

3—Sumner's motion to amend S. 351 by inserting, "That in all judicial proceedings ... there shall be no exclusion of any witness on account of color."

4—Sherman's amendment to S. 394, inserting, "who ... shall owe service or labor to any person who, ... levied war or has borne arms against the United States ..."

5—Sumner's amendment to S. 365, providing for emancipation in the state of West Virginia.

6—King's amendment to the confiscation bill, S. 151, inserting, "persons in the present insurrection levying war against the United States or adhering to their enemies ..."

Expression of such differences appeared in the correspondence of the senators. Writing to Chandler after the close of the second session and as the election of 1862 neared, Wilkinson worried only about the success of ultra-Radicals like himself. Trumbull, as he reviewed the Illinois election for Chandler's benefit a few weeks later, remarked sarcastically: "Do you think it will be any loss to exchange Browning for a responsible Democrat?" To Browning, after the Thirty-seventh Congress had ended, Harris lamented that the President had "been drawn into the views" unfortunately "of a miserable lot of politi-

cians"; a "lot" of which the New Yorker obviously did not consider himself a member.

Most of the eighty-seven roll calls on slavery and confiscation motions fit into six Guttman scales. Beginning at the end of these scales which, judging by the content of the motions, represented the most extreme position relative to slavery and confiscation, I calculated the mean percentile positions of the senators in each scale and then prepared a weighted average of each senator's various scale positions. The average mean-percentile score of both Wilmot and Wade was nineteen, but the score of Senator Powell, a slave state Democrat at the other end of the political spectrum, was eighty-two. The other senators ranged between these poles, Radical Republicans presumably giving way to Moderate Republicans and War Democrats until finally the most conservative representatives of the border slave states were reached.[6] Table I presents the scale pattern found most frequently in the votes on slavery and confiscation.

A rank-order list of this sort derived from Guttman scaling tells us (if we accept the assumptions of the scaling technique) that one senator was more extreme in his approach to a category of legislation than was another, but it does not divide the legislators into self-conscious groups. Some scholars have tried to solve this problem by dividing scale rankings into thirds or by designating one or more votes within a scale as boundaries. Both systems are arbitrary and I have instead worked out cluster blocs, using the percentages of agreement between every possible pair of senators in the voting on the eighty-seven roll calls on slavery and confiscation in my original selection. Such agreement scores

[6] Some students have tried to summarize the voting positions of legislators by summing or averaging their scale type positions in a number of appropriate scales. Unfortunately, such procedure disregards the fact that Guttman scales are ordinal scales and we cannot be sure that the scale types in various scales are equivalent units of measurement. Here, therefore, I have calculated the number of percentiles that the legislators of each scale type occupied and allocated the mean percentile score to each man in the scale type. Such percentile values can, of course, be averaged with those derived from other scales. Actually, the rank ordering of senators derived in this way did not vary greatly from the rank order which resulted when I summed the scale types of the various legislators, although there were some minor differences. But one should not assume that the rank order derived by summing scale types in some published research is inaccurate simply because of the methods used. The results may or may not be correct. I am indebted to Professor Aage Clausen of the Political Science Department of the University of Wisconsin for assistance with this problem.

showed considerable harmony among senators like King, Wilmot, Wilkinson, Chandler, and Wade, who stood at the Radical end of the scalogram rank order, and a considerably lower agreement among these men and a group which included Fessenden, Foster and a few other New Englanders who also agreed among themselves very strongly and appeared in the center of the scaling rank order. We can regard these two groups in a sense as the nuclei of the Radical and Moderate Republicans, with other senators forming an outer fringe in both factions. The boundaries of these groups suggested a cutting point in the scale ranking that yielded seventeen Radicals and fourteen Moderates. In this division the marginal Radicals agreed in their voting with the other Radicals substantially more than with the Moderates. (See Table IIa)

Having divided the Republicans into Radicals and Moderates by using the scales and cluster blocs found in the original selection of eighty-seven roll calls on slavery and confiscation, I could then compute the index of disagreement of each of the 368 roll calls under study. In all there were fifty-eight roll calls in which the disagreement ranged between forty and one hundred. These fifty-eight roll calls delimit the areas of major conflict between Moderate and Radical Republicans in the Senate during the second session.

Much of the disagreement between Radical and Moderate Republicans was, of course, related to emancipation and to the methods by which this might be achieved. During the discussion of Senate Bill 108, providing for the emancipation of slaves in the District of Columbia, Davis of Kentucky proposed that all individuals who were freed under this act should be colonized and that an appropriation should be made for that purpose. Doolittle moved to amend this, allowing all of the freed men

Table II

Republican Radicals and Moderates

Radicals		*Moderates*	
Chandler (Mich.)	Morrill (Me.)	Anthony (R.I.)	Foster (Conn.)
Clark (N.H.)	Pomeroy (Kan.)	Browning (Ill.)	Harris (N.Y.)
Foot (Vt.)	Sumner (Mass.)	Collamer (Vt.)	Howe (Wis.)
Grimes (Ia.)	Trumbull (Ill.)	Cowan (Penn.)	H. S. Lane (Ind.)
Hale (N.H.)	Wade (O.)	Dixon (Conn.)	Sherman (O.)
Harlan (Ia.)	Wilkinson (Minn.)	Doolittle (Wis.)	Simmons (R.I.)
Howard (Mich.)	Wilmot (Penn.)	Fessenden (Me.)	Ten Eyck (N.J.)
King (N.Y.)	Wilson (Mass.)		
J. H. Lane (Kan.)			

Table IIa

Some Radical and Moderate Republican Agreement Scores*

	King	Wilmot	Wilkinson	Chandler	Wade	Morrill	Sumner	Collamer	Foster	Anthony	Simmons	Fessenden
King												
Wilmot	97											
Wilkinson	96	98										
Chandler	94	90	91									
Wade	93	93	96	90								
Morrill	89	91	94	88	89							
Sumner	89	86	89	90	81	92						
Collamer	69	63	66	67	74	78	69					
Foster	68	62	68	69	71	81	72	95				
Anthony	68	64	65	69	72	74	71	92	91			
Simmons	55	58	59	55	60	74	61	90	91	93		
Fessenden	68	67	68	67	68	85	74	87	90	86	95	
Cowan	42	36	34	46	39	44	48	69	65	77	71	63

*Per cent agreement in 87 votes on slavery and confiscation; absences are ignored. The cluster-bloc pairing suggests that the Radical who was closest in his voting to the Moderates was Senator Clark, whose average agreement with the men above him in the matrix (the other Radicals) was 83 per cent, and with the Moderates 77 per cent. The scalogram percentile rankings drop Howard below Clark. Howard's mean pairing score with other Radicals was 80 per cent and with the Moderates only 65 per cent. Such variation is attributable to the fact that absences are handled somewhat differently in the cluster-bloc and scaling procedures and to the fact that the mean percentile method of ranking is by no means precise since large numbers of tie scores are involved. The only senator to present a real problem in classification was Senator Dixon. Historians usually consider him a Moderate, as he apparently did himself, but both scaling and clustering procedures ranked him among the Radicals. When a cluster-bloc matrix was prepared that counted absences as a third way of agreement between legislators, Dixon's average agreement with the Radicals fell to less than 60 per cent, although it was still somewhat higher than his average agreement with the Moderates. Dixon apparently absented himself on some embarrassing roll calls and I have therefore counted him among the Moderates, although this imparted a slightly conservative bias to the calculation of the index of disagreement between Radicals and Moderates.

of the District to choose whether or not they wished to emigrate. His amendment specified Haiti or Liberia as the destination of the emigrants or "such other country ... as the President of the United States" might determine, and limited the expenditures in each individual case to $100. The vote on both the Doolittle amendment and on the amended Davis amendment provoked substantial disagreement between Radicals and Moderates.

In the debate on Senate Bills 384 and 394, to amend the act calling forth the militia, Grimes offered an amendment designed to free the mother, wife and children of those of African descent who served the Union under the amended law, as well as the colored soldier or laborer himself. Moderate colleagues and Border State men opposed this amendment, suggesting that it should apply only to the slaves of traitors, that it should not touch the slaves of loyal slaveowners, or at least that loyal owners in the Border States should be recompensed for losses under it. Eight roll calls on various aspects of this matter produced disagreement of considerable strength. In a more direct blow at the institution of slavery in the Border States, Sumner tried to amend the West Virginia admission act by striking the limited emancipation clause, which provided that all children were to be born free, and substituting the provision that there should be neither slavery nor involuntary servitude in the new state except as criminal punishment. The ringing language of the Northwest Ordinance and of the Wilmot Proviso may have stirred proud nostalgia in many a Republican heart but not one Moderate voted for it.

Various divisive motions related to the disabilities of color, although the implications of the roll calls doubtless ran deeper on occasion. As Senator Clark tried, by amendment, to substitute the select committee version of the confiscation bill in place of the confiscation bill from the House, Sumner attempted to add the words "and in all proceedings under this act there shall be no exclusion of any witness on account of color," to one clause of the senate bill. Almost a full complement of Radicals supported Sumner's amendment and the Moderates massed in opposition to it. When Sumner also tried to attach this amendment both to House Bill 390, "in relation to the competency of witnesses in trials of equity and admiralty," and to a senate bill relating to the judiciary, he encountered strong Moderate opposition in the first instance and less in the second. Radical faced Moderate again when the senators voted on the Border State proposition to amend a naval appropriations bill by barring the use of slaves on the works of the naval service.

The Republican senators disagreed sharply among themselves in the debates on confiscation during the last four months of the session. The discussion focused first on the Trumbull bill, S. 151, which the Illinois senator reported from the judiciary committee. A compromise measure, S. 310, which a select committee under the chairmanship of Senator Clark drafted was considered next and then House Bill 471. Due mainly to the efforts of Moderates, aided by votes from the Border States, the Senate used the amendment process to substitute S. 310 for the bill from the House. Two major questions were involved in the debates: (1) Could Congress reach the property of rebels under powers opened to it by the war crisis or must it be bound by constitutional restrictions on the punishment of treason? (2) What categories of southerners ought to lose their property under the law? The Radicals in general supported the broad application of a law based on the war power; most Moderates fought for judicial processes which they believed were in accord with the treason clause of the constitution and wished to specify limited categories of southerners to whom the law was to apply. Senators introduced various major amendments during the debates and the parliamentary maneuvering was reflected in numerous disagreements between the Radicals and Moderates on procedural matters. In sum, the members of the two groups disagreed substantially in eleven roll calls during the debates on confiscation and the conflict persisted even into the vote on a motion that the Senate withdraw its amendment to the House Bill after the House had asked for a conference committee.

The division between Moderates and Radicals sometimes was revealed in the discussion of matters that at first glance do not relate directly to slavery or confiscation. A bloc of Moderates supported Senator Davis when he tried to amend House Bill 371, "to prescribe an oath of office . . .," so as to exempt congressmen from its operation. Moderates in some number also supported Henderson's amendment to the same bill, changing the affirmation, ". . . I have never voluntarily borne arms against the United States . . .," by striking "borne arms" and replacing it by the phrase "levied war." When Sumner tried to amend the internal revenue bill by inserting an additional section that taxed slave holders at the rate of $5.00 for each slave between the ages of ten and sixty, his action inspired a flurry of opposition and counter-proposals which generated substantial disagreement between the Republican factions. So, too, did the effort of John Sherman to win reconsideration of a 50 per cent reduction in the cotton tax and Sumner's attempt to strike the tax on book-making materials.

The Radicals and Moderates disagreed in four votes dealing with the seating of Benjamin Stark, the Copperhead senator who replaced Baker of Oregon. A similar division appeared in four roll calls relating to the organization, or emoluments, of the armed forces. It was seen also when Senator Harris attempted to have Senate Bill 200, to establish provisional governments in certain cases, made a special order; on an amendment of Senator Grimes to Senate Bill 89, changing the boundaries of Federal judicial districts; in the case of two votes relating to the water and gas utilities of the District of Columbia; on Trumbull's motion to strike the second section of the extradition treaty with Mexico; and on a motion of Hale concerning the dead letter office. Finally, as the legislators reached mid-June, 1862, the same pattern of Radical in opposition to Moderate appeared in seven votes concerning adjournment and the operation of the Senate rules.

The disagreement indices provide us with some evidence of the duration as well as the intensity of disagreement during the session. Three votes revealed substantial disagreement between Radicals and Moderates during January of 1862 but in June there were nineteen, and in considerably less than a month of debate during July, there were seventeen such confrontations. However, every vote in which the index rose to eighty-five or better occurred in July. Party harmony was obviously in serious jeopardy as the session closed. Although we are tempted to emphasize the confiscation issue and the emancipation of slaves in the District of Columbia in discussing the achievements of Congress during this session, the sharpest disagreement between Radicals and Moderates did not develop in the roll calls on these measures but rather when the senators voted on the emancipation clause of the bills to amend the act calling forth the militia and on Sumner's amendment to provide unlimited emancipation in the new state of West Virginia. The votes on these issues produced disagreement indices that ranged from eighty-five to one hundred.

Although the senators might have explained their differences in terms of constitutional interpretation or conscience, we, as historians, inevitably ask ourselves if the differences between Radical and Moderate Republicans are explainable in terms of the conditioning which these men experienced in the years before the Civil War. Ralph Waldo Emerson was playing this game when he wrote in his journal:

The Unitarians, born Unitarians, have a pale, shallow religion, but the Calvinist, born and reared under his vigorous, ascetic, scowling creed, and then ripened into a Unitarian, becomes powerful ... So it is in politics. A man must have had the broad, audacious Democratic party for his nursing-mother, and be ripened into a Free-Soiler, to be efficient. . . .

Emerson's "Law" does have some predictive value when applied to the Republican senators of this session. Of seven former Democrats among the Republicans, six were Radicals, including four of the most Radical complexion, and only Doolittle was a Moderate. Among the senators of Whig antecedents, men who had made some striking commitment to the antislavery cause before 1854 seem in general to have been more extreme than those who made their public commitment in 1854 or thereafter.

In distinguishing between Radicals and Moderates you will remember that I have not arbitrarily selected one or several votes and posited that all who voted one way or another on this limited selection were Radicals or Moderates. Instead I have been concerned with voting frequencies over a rather considerable number of roll calls. This reflects my feeling that it is unreasonable to expect the members of even a closely knit faction to vote together all of the time. And the high disagreement roll calls provide numerous examples of deviation.

Sherman, seldom, if ever, considered a Radical, pressed doggedly for the more severe House version of the confiscation bill in preference to the select committee's compromise measure. Of the Radicals, only Wade joined the Moderates in opposition to Sumner's amendment to the West Virginia admission bill although he termed his vote "very harsh and unsavory." The lion could on occasion lie down with the lamb.

Was there any relation between the sectionalism of East and West and the disagreement between the Radicals and Moderates in the Republican party? We have already noted that east-west sectionalism was most apparent in the voting on national economic issues, but in a number of votes relating to the South there was some alignment of western Republicans in opposition to eastern Republicans. There are various ways of examining this question. If the Republican Radicals were primarily eastern or western in constituency, roll calls showing a high sectional disagreement between eastern and western men should also have a high index of disagreement between Radicals and Moderates. Ten roll calls are common to the list of forty-six votes in which eastern and western Republicans differed substantially and the group of fifty-eight roll calls that show substantial disagreement between Radicals and Moderates.

We can attack the problem more simply by examining the division of eastern and western Republican senators between the Radical and Moderate factions of the party. Table III shows that slightly more than half of the eastern Republicans were Moderates and a somewhat larger proportion of western Republicans were Radicals. Antislavery sentiment in the West is sometimes linked to eastern origins and Table IV presents place of birth as a possible variable.

For what it is worth, the Republican

Table III*

Sections and Radicalism

	Radicals		Moderates	
Eastern Republican Senators (17)	8	47%	9	53%
Western Republican Senators (14)	9	64%	5	36%

*The contingency coefficient gamma is −.34.

Table IV*

Birth and Radicalism

	Radicals		Moderates	
Republican Senators of Eastern Birth (26)	15	58%	11	42%
Republican Senators of Western Birth (5)	2	40%	3	60%

*Gamma is .34 again.

senator most apt to be extreme in his views toward the South and its institutions was a western senator of eastern origins; seven of the nine senators who fitted this description were Radicals (78 per cent). The senator most apt to be a Republican Moderate on the other hand was a western senator of western birth; three out of five, or 60 per cent, in this category were Moderates. But given the relatively small numbers of men involved, the percentage differences that support a sectional interpretation of the disagreement between Radicals and Moderates are rather small.

The fact that there were proportionately more Radicals in the West has sometimes made it difficult for historians to decide whether the sectionalism of East and West or the division between Radicals and Moderates most influenced a particular vote. The sectional aspect of the voting on the colonization amendment to the bill providing for emancipation of the slaves in the District of Columbia has been emphasized recently but roll call analysis seems to show that we should more appropriately view the issue as an aspect of factionalism between Radical and Moderate Republicans in the Senate.

Historians have toyed with the idea that the Republican Radicals not only agreed strongly among themselves on southern policy but that they were peculiarly the spokesmen of northeastern industrialism. We have in general rejected this thesis in recent years and there is little support for it in this research. We can, however, argue that some Republican senators agreed strongly with each other during the second session of the Thirty-seventh Congress both in their voting on slavery and confiscation and on the national economic program of the Republican party. Men like Fessenden, Collamer, Foster, and Anthony tended to agree much of the time, whether the subjects under debate were slavery and confiscation or economic measures of national import. Agreeing strongly with them on economic matters were some of the marginal Radicals from New England, particularly Foot and Clark. If any group of senators can be described as consistently cohesive it was the nucleus of New England Moderates.

Having examined some of the dimensions of geographical bloc and party faction, we can return to the question of whether the historian is justified in emphasizing the internecine conflicts of the Republicans or whether he should stress rather the importance of party and the basic agreement among Republicans. We have seen that eastern and western Republicans differed substantially in forty-six roll calls and that Radical Republican similarly opposed Moderate Republican in fifty-eight votes, with some overlap in the categories. By comparison, the Republican and Democratic parties differed by 40 per cent or more of the total disagreement possible in 161 roll calls. Restating the matter in slightly different terms, a majority of Republicans opposed a majority of Democrats in 180 of the 368 voting divisions. Of the eighty-seven roll calls in my original selection of votes on slavery and confiscation, sixty-five showed a majority of Republicans opposed to a majority of Democrats, and only twenty-one revealed a disagreement index between Moderate and Radical Republicans of substantial size. In these crude terms party was indeed more important than factionalism.

We cannot leave the matter there, however. Howard W. Allen and Jerome M. Clubb calculated the amount of party voting in a total of some twelve hundred votes on the most controversial issues considered in the senates of the Sixty-first, Sixty-second and Sixty-third Congresses, 1909-1915, when the winds of progressivism were blowing strongly. Since Allen and Clubb sifted out some votes on less controversial matters and I considered all roll calls the comparison cannot be exact, but the percentage ranged from 60 to 79 per cent in those congresses, with a mean of 71 per cent. In the second session of the sen-

ate of the Thirty-seventh Congress the percentage of party votes in the selection of eighty-seven roll calls on slavery and confiscation issues was seventy-five but this figure drops to 50 per cent when all 368 roll calls are considered. Relatively speaking, party was apparently less significant in the voting of this session than on the more important issues of Progressivism. On the other hand, "party votes," as a percentage of all Senate votes, represented only 45 per cent on the average during the Eighty-fourth through the Eighty-eighth Congresses, 1955-1964.

Yet, if party lines were drawn very sharply on the issues of slavery and confiscation during the second session of the Thirty-seventh Congress, one out of every four roll calls on such matters did reveal substantial disagreement between Republican Radicals and Moderates. Traces of this division appeared in many other votes as well. Basically, the differences between Radical and Moderate structured the voting of Republicans in one major category of legislation and also affected a number of other types of legislative action that were only indirectly related to the southern question. Nor should we forget that the division between Radical and Moderate was a more important one than was the distinction between eastern and western legislators.

The relative cohesion of the Democrats and the Republicans has some bearing on the significance of party among the Republicans. In a recent article Leonard Curry has argued that the Democrats were more cohesive during the Thirty-seventh Congress than were the Republicans. My voting analysis of the second session Senate supports his conclusion. The mean Democratic cohesion in my original selection of slavery and confiscation votes was sixty-nine and that of the Republicans was sixty-three. In eighty-six divisions on the major national economic legislation of this session, Democratic cohesion was sixty-six and that of the Republicans was thirty-eight. We have to discount this finding somewhat, however, because the Democratic group was small and absenteeism among its members much more marked than among the Republicans, even after adjustment is made for the illness of several Democratic senators.

To divide the roll calls of this session into those that show sectionalism, those that illustrate the conflict of Radical against Moderate Republican, and those that illustrate party differences is to disregard a considerable number of votes. There were 132 roll calls (again with some overlapping of other categories) in which Republican cohesiveness was sixty or below and in which the likeness indices of East against West and of Radical versus Moderate were quite high. In these divisions, apparently, the idiosyncracies of the individual constituency or senator were asserted or subregional voting patterns became important. Although it is possible to build some scales from these roll calls, the scalograms include a relatively small number of votes and it is difficult to identify underlying continua of attitude. As I move further into the task of calculating correlations between the various scales I may be able to refine my description of these votes.

In this session of the Civil War Senate, party obviously was an important voting determinant but we cannot disregard the significance of geographical bloc or party faction either, nor the importance of the individual senator and his constituency.

And, of course, the decision to vote in sectional grouping or party faction may have come only after much agonizing deliberation. Obviously there is much to be said in support of the interpretations of both David Donald and T. Harry Williams concerning Republican factionalism, but we will profit, I believe, in the future by treating the houses of Congress during the Civil War as political systems in which a variety of determinants of voting behavior were interacting.

This particular senate was hardly a classic illustration of the two-party system at work, with its strong Republican majority, its reeling Democracy, its homeless border Unionists and the unusual pressures of constituency and public opinion that played upon the senators. Comparison with a one-party legislature or a multiparty system may be more revealing than exposition of the conventional two-party model. But party objectives were by no means forgotten; Democrats hoped for a comeback and many Republicans had both the present and the future in mind as they labored during this session. The doctrinaire Hale scoffed that the department of agriculture bill was not the wish of the men who leaned "upon their plow-handles; but ... the men who want them to take their hands off the plow-handle and vote for them at the ballot-box." The more practical politicians of the new party prevailed against such criticism and the Thirty-seventh Congress bequeathed a formidable legislative legacy to the people of a reunited nation.

According to WOOD GRAY (b. 1905), professor of history at George Washington University, the Copperheads were peace-at-any-price Democrats. A minority in the party, but counting important political figures in their ranks, they were strongest in the Middle West. They organized the Northwest Confederacy aimed at withdrawal from the war. By spring 1864, under the leadership of Clement L. Vallandigham of Ohio, a Congressman who had been exiled for obstructing the war, a Northwest Conspiracy had been formed in concert with Confederate authorities. Vallandigham proposed to return to Ohio at the time of Grant's crucial campaign in Virginia. His expected arrest would be the signal for revolt in the Northwest. In the chapter from *The Hidden Civil War* (originally published in 1942) that follows Gray examines the Copperhead movement, stressing the planned armed uprising in the Middle West. What motives does he ascribe to the peace movement? How was it related to the military and political developments in the summer of 1864?*

Wood Gray

The Democrats as Copperheads

The project of an armed uprising against the war was now to be jeopardized from an unexpected, even paradoxical, quarter. Early in the summer of 1864 the military situation took a sharp turn for the worse, with the result that prospects for overthrowing the administration at the polls and replacing it with a President and Congress pledged to peace suddenly became so bright that the use of force to achieve this end seemed unnecessary. As the veteran, powerful, and splendidly equipped armies of Grant and Sherman had begun their concerted offensive in May, few in the North had doubted that

the war was entering the final phase. It had seemed impossible that the Confederacy would be able for long to offer an effective defense against the sheer crushing weight of such forces. But an early blight fell upon their movements. Grant's flanking action from the Wilderness to the James River, marked by unprecedented casualties culminating on June 3 in the slaughter at Cold Harbor, came on June 19 to a standstill in front of Petersburg. Here, in a position like that held by McClellan when the Peninsular campaign had been abandoned two years before, the Army of the Potomac lay powerless,

*From *The Hidden Civil War: The Story of the Copperheads* by Wood Gray. Copyright 1942 by Wood Gray. Reprinted by permission of The Viking Press, Inc. Pp. 170–188.

unable to pierce the elaborate system of forts and entrenchments which Lee had constructed in the months of respite since Gettysburg. Likewise, Sherman's thrusts against the flawless parries of Joe Johnston were blocked at Kenesaw Mountain on June 27. Ahead lay the fortifications about Atlanta, comparable in strength to those of Richmond and Petersburg. The war had become a stalemate. The two great military leaders of the Confederacy were evolving a new type of warfare based on large-scale semi-permanent field entrenchments, prophetic of the Western Front of the First World War.

Lee, always keenly aware of the psychological aspects of war, seized on this moment to give the North a dramatic reminder that the Confederacy was still very much alive. In 1862 he had relieved the pressure on Richmond by sending Stonewall Jackson to threaten Washington. Now to play a similar role he chose General Jubal Early, bald, bent, piercing-eyed, whose shrill treble was reputed to be capable of the most lurid profanity in the Confederate army. In spite of his almost legendary eccentricity Early, who opposed secession in 1861 but afterward became such an "unreconstructed rebel" that he would go to his grave without having taken an oath of submission, was a first-rate fighting man. With such troops as Lee could spare he dashed down the Shenandoah Valley, swept through Hagerstown and Frederick, and in the second week of July entered the District of Columbia, which had been stripped of its defenders to reinforce Grant. The Northern capital, it appeared, was more in danger than the Southern. Although repelled by the last-minute arrival of troops sent back from Grant's army, the Confederate force succeeded in making a leisurely and unimpeded return to the Shenandoah Valley, laden with prisoners and booty. The whole episode seemed a

final demonstration of the clumsiness and ineptitude of the leadership of the Northern forces. Hopes had been equally bright in the spring of 1862, and incompetence had dissipated them. Was the story to be repeated? Millions in the North began to wonder.

On June 7, before the full reaction to military reverses was felt, the Union Republican convention, meeting at Baltimore, had renominated Lincoln. The popular conviction still persisting at that time that the war could best be carried on under the existing experienced leadership had made the nomination possible, for without it the fabulously clever wire-pulling of Lincoln and his political henchmen could hardly have been successful. It had been accomplished, however, in the face of powerful opposition, and certain of the sharp expedients that had been employed to bring it about had left many of the other party leaders nursing rancorous and rebellious feelings. Beneath the apparent unity of the convention there were emotions that needed only some marked setback to the administration to effect their release. Before the convention one of Senator Trumbull's constituents had attempted to analyze the state of opinion as he observed it:

...The fact is the people are not satisfied with the loose way in which the war is carried on. Yet they dare not say much and they hardly dare change, yet it would take but little to throw them into confusion and loose [*sic*] us the election. If the democrats nominate McClellan and we nominate Mr. Lincoln and some of the dissatisfied start out on Butler or Fremont we should be whipped. . . .

The change in the military situation now constituted an ideal precipitant for discontent within the Republican fold. Democratic prospects brightened.

Not only were the chances of Democratic success increased; the peace faction within that party was strengthened. The change in sentiment was illustrated by developments in Ohio. When the state convention had met at Columbus on March 23 to choose delegates-at-large, the general expectation of Union victory lent cautiousness to the stand taken on the question of peace. A non-committal platform had been adopted and the general state delegation selected was dominated by moderates. But, when the time came for the picking of delegates from each congressional district, the military outlook was becoming daily more gloomy and the result was that these more popularly chosen representatives were men generally identified with the peace faction. Many of the district conventions adopted at the same time positive declarations against the war. The resolutions of the Ninth (Sandusky) District called for immediate peace; the convention of the Eleventh, meeting at Portsmouth, specifically instructed its delegates to support none but peace candidates and peace measures in the national convention; that of the Fourteenth at Ashland voted that "the delegates to the National Democratic Convention from this Congressional District are hereby instructed to use all honorable means as delegates to the Chicago Convention, to secure the nomination only of peace candidates upon a peace platform, for the Presidency and Vice Presidency of the United States"; and the Fourth District meeting at Piqua adopted a statement of belief that there existed in the federal government no constitutional power to use force against a sovereign state. Vallandigham and former Governor Thomas H. Seymour of Connecticut were understood to be looked upon with most favor as possible candidates by the peace element of Ohio. The *Crisis,* unequivocating advocate of peace at any cost, was sent into raptures. Under the heading "OHIO FOR PEACE—THE PEOPLE HAVE SPOKEN AND THE VICTORY IS WON!" the

editor wrote, "Let the Democrats of Ohio rejoice—let the friends of Peace everywhere rejoice, that Ohio will stand in the Chicago Convention almost unanimous for PEACE—a peace candidate and a peace platform." From an examination of the list of the delegates selected it appeared to the editor that no more than eight would support Representative S. S. Cox's plan of nominating General McClellan and adopting a platform condemning the abandonment of the war but favoring the calling of a peace convention while the fighting continued. The remaining thirty-six, possibly more, were believed to be committed to the peace view, and included such men as Vallandigham, Chilton A. White, Medary himself, Edson B. Olds, Archibald McGregor, and Alexander Long. The editorial concluded, "Ohio may, therefore, be set down as triumphantly for the peace policy, and as goes Ohio, so will go the Union."

To add volume to the expression of their wishes the peace men called local meetings throughout the Midwest to declare their opposition to any equivocation on the question of continuing the war. The Democratic Club of Galena, Jo Daviess County, Illinois, unanimously voted approval of the position taken by Alexander Long and announced "that it is to such men we look for leadership!" ... A convention of the Hendricks County, Indiana, Democrats heard Harrison H. Dodd, commander of the Sons of Liberty in that state, advance the proposal of a Northwest Confederacy as a temporary expedient looking to a reunion with the South. Dodd threatened civil war if the administration should attempt military interference with this or any other action which the Democratic party should attempt to achieve through the regular channels of politics. Many gatherings of this type were reported in Ohio. The Democrats of Jackson Township, Jackson County, adopted resolutions warning that they would support none but peace candidates; a joint gathering from Franklin, Licking, and Delaware counties, held at Columbus on July 23, heard speakers urge the people not to submit to further conscription and to resort to insurrection if arbitrary arrests were resumed, and listened to promises that regardless of whether a peace or war man were elected president "we will never consent to the prosecution of this war"; and a great peace meeting at Bucyrus, Crawford County, resolved its opposition to further conscription and insisted that the war should be no longer continued. Actions of the same nature were reported by meetings in Union, Delaware, Athens, Stark, and Ashland counties.

The anti-war press also swung into action in the old familiar way—reveling in reports of checks, disasters, and slaughter visited upon the Union armies, describing each with loving detail, exaggerating reverses and casualties, giving credence to rumors of disasters about to overtake Grant and Sherman, and insinuating that the troops were ripe for mutiny. It slyly suggested, in contrast to this dismal prospect, that the South would be willing to listen to a reasonable proposal for reunion. . . . The Chicago *Times* of August 1 concluded that a Northwest Confederacy might well be the result of almost inevitable defeat:

The continuance of this war on present terms is as certain to result in the independence of the seceded States as night and day are to follow each other. It is just as certain that the different sections of the Republic, after one extended division, will ally themselves with such portions as can and will most practically assist in the advancement of their respective interests.

Another factor complicated the reigning uncertainty. On July 19, 1864, the President issued a call for 500,000 additional volunteers, deficiencies on assigned quotas to be drafted on September 5. All the obstacles to recruiting that had been increasing during the previous two years were by now fully developed. Democrats sought to discredit the call by charging it with discrimination against the Midwestern states. The La Crosse *Democrat* snarled, "If the people of Wisconsin were not natural born cowards . . . if they were not as great slaves as the blacks this war is now being conducted to benefit, they would stand shoulder to shoulder and swear by the living God that not a man nor a dollar should be sent to war from the West until the East had filled her quotas." . . .

Although high bounties were offered and contributions were being received for the relief of the families of those enlisting, such inducements were counterbalanced by the attraction of greatly increased civilian wages, even farm hands being paid from $2 to $5 a day in the harvest field. The public was apathetic and volunteering was meager—a fact not only apparent from the statistics but implicit in charges going back and forth that recruiting agents were attempting to lure men from other states, in the efforts being made to get quotas decreased, and in authorization for the enlistment of rebel prisoners. Governor Brough of Ohio begged the Secretary of War, "For the first time in my varied and extensive official correspondence with you I ask a reduction of the military forces you demand from Ohio."

It was readily apparent that the greater part of the call would have to be filled by drafting, and state and federal officials were agreed that this task would have to be performed in the face of possible widespread resistance. Governor Brough feared that from 10,000 to 15,000 soldiers might be required to enforce conscription in Ohio. . . . The problem had aspects other than the danger of armed resistance. Republicans feared and Democrats hoped that the unpopularity of a draft carried out at the height of a political campaign would insure Lincoln's defeat. And, finally, there was the question whether men so opposed to entering the army as to require such a force to compel them to serve would have any worth as soldiers.

Again, as in the campaign of 1862, the Republicans, faced by widespread discontent among the people and an aggressive Democratic attack, seemed more intent on quarreling among themselves than on preserving a united front against the common enemy. The congressional radicals had tried hard to prevent Lincoln's renomination. . . . Lincoln's hold on the imagination of the Republican masses and his clever, and not infrequently ruthless, manipulation of party machinery succeeded in bringing about his renomination by the national convention with the open opposition of only one state delegation, that of Missouri, but the radicals, foreseeing an approaching struggle over reconstruction as well as nursing resentments for past disagreements, could muster little enthusiasm for the ticket.

As the summer wore on and the unpromising military outlook was re-emphasized by each day's news, even the popularity that Lincoln had built up among the common people began to fade, not so much taking the shape of specific criticisms of the administration as manifesting itself in a general dejection that seemed ready to admit the hopelessness of the war policy that it was attempting to pursue. . . . Military victories would be likely to dissipate much of this feeling, but further defeats would greatly augment its strength. A potentially dangerous factor in the situation was the Fremont ticket. At the time of the nomination of the Republican candidate of 1856 by a haphazard convention of malcontents at Cleveland on May 31, 1864 this ticket had been something of a joke. But in the

developments of the next three months it came increasingly to be feared that disgruntled elements, particularly the Germans, marshaled by the St. Louis *Missouri Democrat* and their own language press, might support him in such numbers as to effect not his election but the defeat of Lincoln by the Democratic candidate.

The issuance of the Wade-Davis Manifesto on August 5, 1864, savagely denouncing Lincoln for his conciliatory reconstruction policy, added to the dissension, and nine days later a further division seemed about to take place. On the 14th day of August a meeting of New York journalists and others, including David Dudley Field, Congressman Henry Winter Davis, and Professor Francis Lieber, took stock of the situation. Agreeing that Lincoln's chances were hopeless, they decided to issue a private call for a new national convention to be held in Cincinnati on September 28, at which Lincoln would be replaced by a more promising candidate. Salmon P. Chase, who had petulantly resigned from the cabinet after Lincoln's renomination, was being urged by many of his supporters to bolt the Union ticket and had returned answers that led some to believe that he might be prevailed upon to accept an independent nomination for the presidency. With discouragement general, with Horace Greeley badgering him through the widely read *Tribune* to attempt a negotiated peace, and his own party apparently disintegrating into mutually repellent factions, Lincoln had little reason to be in any way hopeful for the future. On August 23 he secretly recorded the conviction that his re-election and the victorious conclusion of the war were unlikely if not impossible.

On the other hand the revolutionary designs of the Sons of Liberty and their secret allies had been suffering repeated setbacks. First, Vallandigham's return to Ohio in the middle of June failed to provide the expected occasion for rising because the Washington authorities decided, after some hesitation, not to order his arrest. The next occasion chosen was the meeting of the Democratic national convention, scheduled for July 4 in Chicago, and that was spoiled by the postponement of the convention. July 16 was then selected, it being expected that opponents of the war would be stirred up by a new call for troops. But the Copperhead leaders were showing definite signs of loss of nerve and their lack of preparation and co-ordination was becoming increasingly apparent. The arrest of some of the principal "S.O.L.'s" in Kentucky, after their return from conferences in Canada with the Confederate representatives, was definitely disturbing and created a fear that spies and informers were learning their secrets. Accordingly the leaders of the Sons of Liberty were forced to report to their Confederate friends that further devices for arousing the public mind would have to be provided before an uprising could be brought about. On June 22, at a conference between the Copperheads and the Southern agents at St. Catharines, Ontario, their plans were redrafted and preparations were made to stage a series of huge demonstrations for peace at Peoria, Springfield, and Chicago, successively. The meeting at Chicago on August 16 was to be the occasion for the revolt, simultaneous gatherings being arranged for other cities on the same date. Jacob Thompson paid over large sums to be used to defray the transportation costs involved. The attendance at the Peoria meeting was gratifying, and the people applauded the sentiments of the principal speaker, Amos Green of Edgar County, who was in charge of the military preparations of the Sons of Liberty in Illinois:

There is no longer a question before us as to whether we can subjugate the South.—The great question with us is, whether we will be able to save from the wreck our own liberties. . . .

Let us no longer crouch at the feet of power with our petitions. Let us stand up and *demand* that the rights and liberties bequeathed us by our fathers be respected, and proclaim if they are not respected, we will maintain them as our fathers achieved them.

On August 15 a smaller gathering at Hamilton, Ohio, adopted resolutions declaring that

the States have the right to withdraw their consent to the Union, and resume their independence, by repealing their ordinance of accession, and passing ordinances of secession. . . . That a State having been withdrawn from the Federation . . . cannot be invaded with a purpose to compel its return. . . .

. . .We but perform a natural and social duty in declaring "to all whom it may concern," that *no citizen of Ohio, resident of Butler county,* shall be compelled to join the Federal army to consummate the avowed designs of the enemies of State rights, even should it prove necessary to give effect to this decision *by force and with arms.*

Resolved that the citizens of this country, who are opposed to a further prosecution of the war, *should prepare for such a contingency.*

And on August 13 a meeting at Fort Wayne, Indiana, resolved "that the honor, dignity, and safety of *the people demand that against ruin and enslavement, they must afford to themselves the protection which usurpation and tyranny denies them.*" One at Iowa City adopted comparable resolutions. But at Peoria and elsewhere it was apparent that in demanding peace and the abandonment of conscription most of the audience looked to political rather than revolutionary activity to achieve these ends.

The rallies at Springfield and Chicago brought out comparatively small crowds and were otherwise discouraging to the revolutionaries. Members of the State Central Committee of the Democratic party in

Indiana, some of whom were or had been members of the Sons of Liberty, acted to head off the attempt of Grand Commander Harrison H. Dodd to have a party mass meeting at Indianapolis on the 16th. They wanted nothing to interfere with a political outlook that was growing daily more promising. On August 13 they issued a public announcement urging people of the state not to resist conscription but to seek redress in political action. In the face of opposition from such sources, the arrests made in Kentucky, and the parallel publication of their rituals and the revelation of some of their activities it was decided that the prospects for a successful *coup d'état* were inauspicious. August 16 came and passed without disturbance.

The Confederate agents, however, were determined not to abandon the project, and another conference was held at London, Canada. The Sons of Liberty still professed to be willing to undertake a revolt if a suitable occasion could be found, and it was agreed that the Democratic national convention at Chicago, finally scheduled for August 29, would offer the most favorable opportunity. This time the Confederates determined to see that the chance should not be wasted and made arrangements to be on hand themselves. About 70 former soldiers of the Confederate armies, under the command of Captains Hines and Castleman, made their way to the convention city. The Copperhead "generals" promised to have 50,000 of their followers present, and Charles Walsh of Chicago had been supplied with funds to equip two regiments of revolutionaries which he claimed to have ready for action in that city. Additional sums were advanced for the purchase of arms and the transportation of the various units of the order, in particular to Amos Green in Illinois, Harrison H. Dodd and John C. Walker in Indiana, and T. C. Massie of

Ohio. At Camp Douglas in Chicago there were nearly 5000 Confederate prisoners. It was hoped that their guard of 1000 men, largely made up of invalids of the Veteran Reserve Corps, could be overpowered and the liberated men armed from the federal arsenal to strike a blow at the vitals of the North. At the signal Southern sympathizers throughout the North were to rise, sever all telegraphic and railway communications, free the prisoners in the other camps of the area, and, if possible, seize control of the governments of the Northwest.

There is no justification for assuming that all these expectations were mere daydreams of overexcited Copperheads. If there were no concerted revolt there might well be local resistance to conscription at many points which could develop into something definitely serious. Both civil and military authorities in the Middle West received reports of heavy shipments of arms into many parts of the region. . . . The problem was so widespread and the resources available for checking it so limited that Governor Yates urged the sending of a considerable body of soldiers to the district and the appointment of a federal military commander for the state. Governor Morton reported a similar state of affairs in southern Indiana, and General Heintzelman admitted that he dared not make military arrests for fear of provoking an uprising which he would not have sufficient force to put down. He also voiced fears for the security of the Confederate prisoners and, with the commander of the Department of the Northwest, General Pope, at Milwaukee, predicted that drafting would provoke resistance beyond the power of the forces stationed in the Midwest to control. Counting up all the demands made upon him for troops for the preservation of order in the Middle West, General Halleck, in one of his few evidences of humor in official correspondence, remarked to Grant, "Add these requisitions to those from New York, Pennsylvania, New Jersey, and Delaware, and I think we can dispose of a few hundred thousand men, if you can spare them from the James River." But he continued, "Seriously, I think much importance should be attached to the representations of General Heintzelman in regard to the condition of affairs in the West." In June, in a message recommending that because of the disturbed conditions in the Middle West the Confederate prisoners be sent to the East, Governor Brough had predicted, "External raids and internal trouble in Indiana and Illinois promise a warm summer's work." As disguised Confederates, armed Sons of Liberty, and Democratic delegates converged on Chicago in the last week of August these threats were apparently approaching fulfillment and the Union seemed menaced by a twofold danger—political and insurrectionary.

The Democratic leaders, eager to be in a position to take the fullest possible advantage of Republican embarrassments, had postponed the meeting of their national convention to the latest practicable date. The deliberations of the convention itself, beginning on August 29, bore witness to the same intent. The military situation still remained such that its final outcome appeared unpredictable, and it would be politic, therefore, to spread a net as broad as possible. Compromise and evasion ruled. A large proportion of the Midwestern delegates, led by the Ohio contingent, had come to the meeting favoring a peace program and nominee, but Governor Horatio Seymour of New York and most of the Eastern men, on the other hand, were certain that such a course would alienate the moderates everywhere and prove fatal to the party in the Northeast. To this group the most desirable and promising

move would be the nomination of General George B. McClellan as the party standard bearer on a platform calling for the prosecution of the war on its original basis (i.e., abandonment of emancipation), meanwhile endeavoring to secure reunion by negotiation. Such an appeal, it was thought, would take the fullest advantage of all shades of dissatisfaction with the incumbent administration. But there remained the danger that the insistent peace elements of the Midwest, if overridden entirely, might carry out threats to bolt the party. Accordingly Vallandigham was approached—so at least was the general understanding about the convention hall—and a bargain arranged. McClellan was nominated for the presidency, although a small block of Ohio and Indiana delegates led by Alexander Long joined with border states delegates in opposing him to the end, peace advocate George H. Pendleton of Ohio was unopposed for the vice-presidency, and the platform was drafted to meet the demands of the peace faction. The crucial second plank of the platform read:

Resolved, That this Convention does explicitly declare as the sense of the American people, that after four years of failure to restore the Union by the experiment of war, during which, under the pretense of a military necessity, or war power higher than the Constitution, the Constitution itself has been disregarded in every part, and public liberty and private rights alike trodden down, and the material prosperity of the country essentially impaired justice, humanity, liberty and the public welfare demand that immediate efforts be made for a cessation of hostilities with a view to an ultimate convention of all the States, or other peaceable means to the end that at the earliest practicable moment peace may be restored on the basis of the Federal Union of the States.

With this statement, which might mean much or nothing, the peace faction had to be content. They were determined that it should mean a great deal. Outside the convention hall they set the tone of the meeting. On street corners semi-impromptu gatherings heard speakers such as Fernando Wood of New York, Vallandigham, Henry Clay Dean of Iowa, and other eccentrics of the stripe of that crank of cranks, George Francis Train, demand immediate and unconditional peace, urge forcible resistance to conscription and arbitrary arrest, and depict the attractiveness of a union in which the Midwest and South would be rejoined but New England excluded. It was evident that the peace men were conscious of their strength and determined that their views should not be ignored in a final settlement after political victory. The rumor circulated among them that McClellan's supporters had agreed to move for peace on any terms as soon as their candidate was safely elected, if only the issue were not pressed during the campaign.

But while the peace Democrats who sought to gain their objectives by political means were winning at least a partial victory, those who looked to revolutionary action had seen the complete failure of their plans. A meeting of the conspirators at the Richmond House in Chicago on August 28 revealed the hopeless outlook for a successful rising. For a number of reasons the commanders of the Sons of Liberty had lost enthusiasm for the project. Their backwoods forces, scattered throughout the town and bewildered by unfamiliar big city surroundings, were neither organized nor nerved for an outbreak. The arrest of their fellow-conspirators in Missouri and Kentucky and a raid in Indiana, instigated by Governor Morton, that had uncovered records, correspondence, and arms of the Sons of Liberty in the office of state Grand Commander Dodd in Indianapolis had resulted in successive depressions of

their confidence and courage. Finally the promise of Democratic victory seemed to make such a hazardous venture unnecessary and ill-advised. Their Supreme Commander, Vallandigham, had been taken back into the councils of the party and now appeared to find his exalted position in the order an embarrassment and liability of which he would be happy to rid himself. Other party leaders in contact with the society brought pressure to prevent any untoward action that might furnish political capital for their opponents. When delegate Edson B. Olds of Ohio sought a hearing in the convention for a communication from the Sons of Liberty he was howled down and induced to abandon his motion. To cap all, the federal authorities, getting wind of the conspiracy, had fortified the garrison at Camp Douglas to a point where a prison break could hardly succeed under the most favorable conditions. Reviewing these circumstances at their conference Confederates and Copperheads agreed that the plot would have to be abandoned. As the convention broke up, the Sons of Liberty returned quietly to their homes, and the Confederate adventurers, knowing that strangers would be conspicuous in the city with the departure of delegates and spectators of the convention, either returned to Canada or else went into hiding with sympathizers in the Middle West.

Although the revolutionary movement had fizzled, the political threat against continuation of the war loomed formidably enough. The Democrats seemed united. In McClellan they had nominated a candidate who would appeal to the war Democrats, both those who had been co-operating for the past three years with the Republicans and those who had remained undeviatingly faithful to the party. He might through his personal popularity and appeal also win considerable numbers of votes from independent sources and perhaps even from discontented Republicans. The peace Democrats, it was expected, would be held in line by the platform and the nominee for the vice-presidency. Declining confidence in the war's outcome, suggested by the fall in value of paper currency to one-third of the price of gold, and other indications of widespread spiritual fatigue seemed to forecast Democratic victory. The Republicans were divided, wrangling and exchanging blame among themselves, and thoroughly discouraged. In a district that in normal circumstances was stanchly Republican one party worker admitted:

...The Democracy are going *unanimously* for McClellan—Lincoln's course has not only dissatisfied but *embittered* many thousands of Republicans, particularly Germans, against him; the Fremont party, and the Chase and Wade-Davis movement, and the anti-slavery dissatisfaction in New England, weakens him greatly; there is no enthusiasm for him, and cannot be, while every saloon, and concert hall will ring and re-echo with songs for McClellan.

And if McClellan were elected, what then? Although classified as a supporter of the war, his susceptibility to the pressure of those about him left room for fears that his personal predilections would be no guarantee that the war would be energetically pursued until the Union should be restored. He would be dependent upon a Congress and state authorities whose support of such a policy seemed at best doubtful. Democratic victories in the state elections of Indiana and Illinois were anticipated, victories essentially for the peace Democrats. A Republican political worker confided:

...I think Indiana is lost for both Lincoln & Morton. I was told at Indianapolis last week by some of Morton's best friends that it was extremely doubtful whether he could carry the

State. There is a dreadful apathy prevailing in all this region of Ohio & nearly all of Indiana. . . .

The Democratic candidate for governor of Illinois, Congressman James C. Robinson, was closely identified with the extreme peace partisans, and during the campaign accepted $40,000 from Jacob Thompson, giving in return assurances which satisfied Thompson that the Confederate interests would be advanced to that extent by his election. One-half of this sum was used to repay an advance to the Illinois Democratic State Central Committee from C. H. McCormick, who may well not have known the source of these funds. A notation in Thompson's official journal for October 24, 1864, recorded:

When Mr. J. A. Barrett of Illinois and B. P. Churchill of Cincinnati visited Mr. Thompson, bringing a letter from Honorable Alex Long, and assurances from Messrs. Vallandigham, Develin of Indiana, Green and Robinson of Illinois, and others, that it was of the last importance to secure the election of Mr. Robinson as governor of Illinois, and asking that money should be advanced for that purpose, stating that Robinson had pledged himself to them, that if elected he would place the control of the militia and the 60,000 stand of arms of that state in the hands of the order of the Sons of Liberty. Mr. Thompson agreed that whenever proper committees were formed of responsible persons to use the money effectually and in good faith to secure that end, that he would furnish the money.

Robinson promptly gave written assurances concerning his objectives as would-be governor in a letter addressed to "Messrs. Green, O'Melveny and others" but apparently intended for Thompson, to whom it was forwarded. It read:

Gentlemen: Your letter of enquiry came duly to hand and its contents noted.

In reply I would state that if elected governor of the state I will see that its sovereignty is

maintained, the laws faithfully enforced and its
citizens protected from arbitrary arrest, and if
necessary for these purposes will, after exhaust-
ing the civil, employ the entire military force of
the state. I will also be happy to avail myself of
the counsel and aid of the executive committee
of the Peace Democracy in the conduct and organization of the militia of the state, recognizing the fact that a well organized militia is necessary for the maintenance of state rights as
well as the liberties of the people. Hoping that
the Democracy may be successful in the great
contest and that Constitutional liberty may
again be reinstated in the full plenitude of her
power, I remain

Yours truly,
James C. Robinson

Even if the national contest were not won,
the Southern emissaries could see promising possibilities in having officials in control of one of two important states who
would withdraw those states from support
of the war. If that should occur, who could
say that the war was yet lost to the South?
On one thing political watchmen of all
varieties seemed to be in agreement, that
on the military events of the next few
weeks depended the outcome of the elections, state and national. Even as the Democrats were choosing their nominee and
writing their platform and the revolutionary conspirators were attempting to decide
upon a course of action, the issue was approaching a decision on the field of battle.
At Atlanta, the economic capital of the
Confederacy, a red-haired, outspoken military genius, General Tecumseh Sherman,
was throwing his enveloping lines around
the city. His success or failure would be the
heaviest ballot cast in the election campaign.

Like Wood Gray, FRANK L. KLEMENT (b. 1908)
concentrates on Middle Western Copperheadism. Unlike
Gray, however, he stresses its economic foundations. The
reader should note Klement's analysis of the sources of
discontent and, in passing, the duration of the discontent.
The two historians' descriptions of the situation in 1864
may be compared. Other points of comparison are: the
Copperheads' pro-southernism, their loyalty to the Union,
and their identification with American traditions. Frank L.
Klement is professor of history at Marquette University,
and author of *The Copperheads in the Middle West* (1960), a
detailed study of this selection's theme.*

Frank L. Klement

The Democrats as Sectionalists

The barometer of popular opinion
gauges Civil War Copperheadism as
cloudy, foul, and pro-Southern. Historians
have encouraged such a rating by reciting
and exploiting the views of the fanatical
fringe, by apotheosizing the Civil War heroes, and by ignoring the forces which underwrote discontent. By disregarding the
environment which produced a corps of
critics and by slighting causation, writers
have tended to look upon Copperheadism
from a legalistic and nationalistic point of
view. But these Midwestern malcontents
did not operate in a vacuum! They represented widespread Western views and
championed Western needs. Economic factors, in part, prompted their prolonged
protests. The severing of West-South ties of
trade, the excessive freight rates levied
upon Western produce shipped eastward,
the economic program of the Northeast,
the nationalization of business, and the
centralization of government induced
them to resurrect Jeffersonian principles to
protect their section and its economy.
They became Western sectionalists because they opposed the increasing power of
Northeastern industrialism, which in seeking its goals threatened the balance of power the West had held politically and the
sectional prosperity they had enjoyed eco-
nomically.

Sectional loyalty characterized most of
the Midwestern Copperheads. Clement L.
Vallandigham's speech in the House of
Representatives entitled, "There Is a

*Frank L. Klement, "Economic Aspects of Middle Western Copperheadism," *The Historian,* XIV (Autumn,
1951), 27–44. Most footnotes omitted.

West," and his contention that he was "as good a Western fire-eater as the hottest salamander in this House" expressed his loyalty to his section. That same Western sectionalism was evident in the fears of those who claimed that the Northeast desired "to subordinate the agriculture of the West to her manufacturing interests." . . .

Secession on the one hand and war on the other threatened the sectional balance, so those Westerners subsequently stigmatized as Copperheads opposed both and advocated compromise in the dreary and disquieting days preceding the surrender of Sumter. The *Cincinnati Enquirer* recited statistics to show the economic interdependence of the Northwest and the South. Medary's editorials in *The Crisis* goaded his readers to support compromise measures. Cyrus H. McCormick regarded the Southern market, and his credits therein, important enough to warrant the purchase of the *Chicago Times* and to conduct a vigorous campaign in behalf of compromise. Vallandigham even submitted a proposal which would allow a vote by sections in the Senate of the United States;[1] thus, the cotton South and the agricultural Northwest could protect their economic interests.

When compromise efforts failed, the same shots which brought about the surrender of Sumter and precipitated the nation into a civil war released an economic depression which ravaged the Northwest and undermined the patriotism evidenced by unfurled flags, marching feet, and emotional oratory. This business plague caused thousands to turn the keys in their office doors during the remaining months of

1861 and file petitions of bankruptcy.[2] That economic panic was a Hydra-headed monster, for the river trade collapsed, bank notes based upon Southern bonds depreciated in value, factory owners lost their Southern markets, and farm prices spiralled downward. The professional classes endured hard times, and the laboring men experienced unemployment.

The commercial interests dependent upon Western-Southern trade suffered as civil conflict severed trade lines. Although the railroad trunk lines extending eastward and the Great Lakes' ports were turning the West from the South, the river trade of 1860 had set an all-time record both as to value and volume. Hundreds of steamboats and thousands of merchants had participated in the river trade, sending large consignments of wheat, whiskey, corn, flour, bacon, poultry, hogs, horses, and merchandise down the river and receiving sugar, molasses, cotton, rice, and tobacco in exchange.[3]

Cincinnati, self-styled "Queen City" and the West's prize river port, entered upon a period of business retrenchment, for the coming of the war brought ruin to many wholesale merchants, shipbuilders,

---

[2]Appleton's *Annual Cyclopedia and Register of Important Events, 1861,* 312, reported 582 business failures in Ohio, 441 in Illinois, 253 in Indiana, and more than 500 in other Midwestern states. The number of failures would have been much higher but two circumstances modified the impact. "One was that the panic of 1857 had weeded out, so to speak, the weakest of the houses, while in November, 1860, when affairs became threatening, the fall trade was passed, stocks of goods on hand were light, and there was little effort to prepare for a large spring business. Hence the payments due in the spring were, to a considerable extent, realized before non-intercourse took place." *Ibid.,* 311–313.

[3]*De Bow's Review,* New Series, I (January, 1861), 253–54, claimed that the states of Arkansas and Mississippi produced very little more than one-fourth of their necessary provisions; they were dependent upon the river trade for the other three-fourths.

---

[1]The Ohioan proposed "to establish four [Northeast, Northwest, South, and Southwest] . . . . grand sections of the Union," giving each section the right to veto Congressional measures in the Senate and assuring each section a voice in the selection of the President.

and steamboat owners as well as unemployment to a host of laborers. "Trade and business everywhere are almost at a standstill," reported an observer in May, 1861. "Hundreds of merchants are weekly closing their business ... and debts are scarcely thought of being paid." The Cincinnati Chamber of Commerce blamed the city's economic plight upon the embargo which ended trade with the South. The editorial columns of the *Enquirer* voiced dissatisfaction with the Lincoln Administration and blamed the Republican party for the troubled times. One of the *Enquirer's* owners, Washington McLean, owned several boiler-plate factories, giving him a special interest in the river trade.

Evansville occupied the position in Indiana which Cincinnati did in Ohio. It was the heart of "The Pocket," and the rivers were its arteries of trade. Lawrenceville, Aurora, Vevay, Madison, New Albany, and Cannelton experienced business distress and saw their mercantile interests prostrate. Cannelton's lucrative stone trade, financed by Louisville capital, prompted a New Year's eve resolution at the end of 1860, that Cannelton be included in the neighboring nation if an international boundary had to be drawn.

Cairo traders, dreaming of making their city America's greatest river port, had seen twelve hundred tons of produce move southward daily late in 1860 and early in 1861. War dealt a death blow to Cairo's roseate dreams and an economic nightmare replaced it. John A. Logan, blusterous and boisterous, spoke the mind of "Egypt" when he denounced Douglas: "You have sold out the Democrat party, but *by God,* you can't deliver it!" The reduction in Cairo's commerce stunned the Illinois Central Railroad, which suffered a financial crisis. Other Illinois rail lines also encountered hardship in the first half of 1861. The Burlington & Missouri Railroad, for example, had its receipts cut in half. Even the Chicago commercial houses felt the effects of the opening of the war. The editor of the *Chicago Times* had earlier written: "In the Union we have our commercial wings stretched North and South, and sail with both...."

The Ohio-Mississippi network funnelled southward many products of various manufactories of the Northwest, and the closing of the trade routes brought hardships and encouraged complaints. Cincinnati, for example, possessed at least nineteen different industries, each of which produced well over a million dollars' worth of goods annually; a considerable portion of the products depended upon a Southern market—eighty-five per cent of the furniture, seventy-seven per cent of the ale and beer, and sixty-three per cent of the whiskey went down the river. McLean, Democratic boss of Hamilton county and political patron of Vallandigham, shipped forty per cent of his boiler plate to Southern purchasers. He resented the competition provided by Pennsylvania ironworks and bemoaned the collapse of his boiler-plate business. Early in the war McLean joined the anti-Administration forces and helped transform the *Enquirer* into one of the most critical and carping Copperhead sheets. The *Enquirer* repeatedly spoke in terms of Western interests and advantage as it tied its own prosperity to that of Cincinnati and Cincinnati's to that of the West.

The McCormicks had a lucrative market for their reapers in Virginia and other Southern states. War measures induced the eldest brother to write: "... our losses South will probably be heavy." Quincy-packed pork usually moved down the Mississippi, and even the Chicago packers sent large quantities of meat southward. Illinois distillers, who owned forty-two plants which produced 15,165,760 gallons of distilled spirits in 1860, were hard hit when the down-river trade dwindled. Dissatisfied distillers provided much of the opposition to the Lincoln Administration in Belleville, Quincy, Chicago, Pekin, and Peoria.[4]

The collapse of the state banking systems of the Northwest aggravated the economic situation and added fuel to the fires of discontent. Bonds of Southern states constituted three-fourths (viz., $9,527,500) of the securities upon which Illinois paper money was based. Secession and war caused the Southern bonds to slide downward and, subsequently, to invalidate the state bank note issues. By November, 1861, only seventeen solvent banks remained in the "Sucker State," whereas 112 had been functioning a year earlier. The currency circulation registered an even sharper decline, from $12,000,000 to $400,000.

Wisconsin banks had relied heavily upon "Missouri Sixes," "North Carolina Sixes," and the state bonds of Louisiana, Virginia, and Tennessee to validate the $4,580,632 worth of state bank notes in circulation in 1860. By July 1, 1861, thirty-eight Wisconsin banks had declared bankruptcy, and a score more tottered on the rim of ruin as Southern bonds depreciated. Financial hocus-pocus, which substituted Wisconsin state bonds for the worthless Southern securities, saved the banks further embarrassment, although this action later received the condemnation of a legislative committee. The banking institutions of other Midwestern states also experienced a crisis.

These bank failures placed a heavy burden upon the struggling economy of the Northwest. There was a shortage of currency to handle the fall harvests. In addi-

tion, much of the direct loss was borne by farmers who held the stock of the defunct banks or who had the depreciating currency passed on to them. A July, 1861, entry in one Illinois farmer's diary told the story: "July 20, 1861—Sold some broken bank money at 35 cts to the $." Workingmen, too, were victims of questionable practices, on occasion being paid in notes of which banks had cleaned their vaults. A bank riot in Milwaukee and public protests in Watertown and Janesville weakened popular support of the Republican state and national administrations.

These readjustments in financial, industrial, and commercial circles drove farm prices downward. In most agricultural sectors corn commanded only ten cents per bushel, and it reportedly sold for as low as seven cents a bushel in western Ohio and six cents in one section of Illinois. Wheat brought less than twenty cents a bushel in many markets. Flour could be bought throughout the West for two or three dollars a barrel. No demand existed for butter or potatoes, while the Chicago quotations on hogs were cut in half in 1861. Some farmers burned their wheat for fuel rather than dispose of it at ruinous prices. The wave of discontent which swept the Northwest in 1862 was rooted in the farmers' economic problems—arrival of interest-paying days, mortgage installments, unwanted agricultural surpluses, and empty pocketbooks.

The European demand for American foodstuffs failed to benefit the Midwestern farmer. The closing of the southward trade routes made the Midwest solely dependent upon the east-west lines of transportation. The Great Lakes–Erie Canal waterways and the railroads leading eastward, many westerners felt, "skinned the West alive." Railroad freight rates were more than doubled during 1861, and the tonnage rates assessed by the carriers on the Great

[4] The five states which made up the Old Northwest contained 233 distilleries in 1860. Production for that year totalled 29,447,395 gallons. Peoria distilleries alone had a daily capacity of 11,650 bushels of grain.

Lakes rose in like manner. Corn commanded a price nearly sixty per cent higher in New York than in Cincinnati. Not only had Illinois farmers lost fifty million dollars in 1861 because of reduced wheat prices, but they paid an additional thirty million in increased freight rates for the year. Farmers' views were aptly expressed by the editor of the *Wisconsin Farmer:*

The farmers work like heroes to produce their great crops of wheat, and then practically give to shipowners and transportation companies . . . all the profits of their toil.

High freight rates helped to spread dissatisfaction throughout the West, gave strength and force to the Copperhead movement, and sowed the seeds of Grangerism, which blossomed into full flower in the 1870's. General John A. McClernand, who toured the West in late 1862 as Lincoln's emissary and election analyst, blamed the political revolt of 1862 upon high freight rates. William H. Osborn, the inquisitive and energetic president of the Illinois Central, who submerged his political views to business activity, recognized that Copperheadism combined sectionalism and economic exigency. He pointed out that in the "two years of war and distress" farmers paid "thirty-five to fifty cents per bushel to get their grain to market," so they had just cause to be malcontents. He added:

The West won't stand the Albany and Buffalo monopoly much longer. A score of canal boat-men combine to get a higher price per bushel for ten days transportation than a farmer gets for toiling and sweating all through the summer months. He plows—they reap. He sows—they gather the harvest. The pressure is getting stronger . . . . A word to the wicked is sufficient.

Prominent critics of the Lincoln Administration—termed "Copperheads" by the Republican party press—continued their Granger-like protests. Vallandigham, whose extremism was ultimately to cause his destruction, claimed that his section paid tribute to the Northeast:

Cut off as we are from all other means of outlet . . . and with our railroads leading to the East, for the most part in the hands of Eastern directors or bondholders, the tariff of freights has at the same time been doubled, thus increasing the burden upon our trade both ways, so largely as to amount in a little while longer to absolute prohibition."

Other complaints against the railroads were added to the list. Westerners charged that the elevators at the Great Lakes' ports were railroad-owned and railroad-operated and that a gigantic monopoly threatened the farmers' life. They claimed that rail rates were discriminatory in that they varied from section to section, favoring some and penalizing others. They resented the promotional practices which unloaded large blocks of railroad stocks and bonds upon local governmental units. They protested against railroad lobbying tactics, which were both sundry and devious. They censured pooling and stock-watering, for both tended to bring about higher rates. Prominent Copperheads, especially in Illinois, occupied the leading role in attacking questionable railroad practices.

Republican-sponsored tariff acts were still another source of grievance to the Midwestern farmer. Household needs as well as durable consumer goods climbed in price, while farm prices plunged downward. To farmers, it did not seem fair to exchange four bushels of corn for a pound of coffee. Vallandigham argued earnestly that the masses, the consumers and farmers, were penalized by protective tariffs; he contended that protection, as a tax, fell heaviest upon those least able to bear it. The *Cincinnati Enquirer* labelled the Northeast's tariff policy as "extremely selfish and injurious to the interests of the North-West." S. D. Carpenter, Wisconsin Copper-head, claimed that the high tariff was "as much a curse to the Great West as the South" and called it "a monster tax" lev-ied "on the Mississippi Valley for the benefit of a few Eastern lords." Frederic W. Horn, Carpenter's colleague in party and politics and three-time speaker of the state senate, resigned his captaincy in the militia rather than fight in a war which, he felt, would assure the sectional domination of New England; so he announced his op-position to a continuation of a Union in which the Middle West was "plundered" for the benefit of "Pennsylvania Iron mon-gers and New England manufacturers." Other prominent opponents of the Lincoln Administration spoke the same language. The editor of the *Milwaukee See-Bote* head-lined a long editorial "The Irrepressible Conflict between East and West" and in-terpreted Copperheadism as a clash of the industrial Northeast and the agricultural Northwest. Medary added his rasping voice to the anti-tariff chorus. S. S. Cox of Ohio anathematized the tariff as "a great fiscal tyranny" by which the West paid a subsidy to "the iron-masters of Pennsylva-nia and the cotton millionaires of New England." Another congressman, speaking for Illinois farmers and emphasizing the sectional aspect of tariff legislation, noted,

Every time we have a nail driven into a horse-shoe, we are taxed; every time we use a wire to ring the snout of a swine, we are taxed; and every time we use a cup of tea we are taxed . . . .

One dejected farmer referred to the tariff as "that ass' jawbone by which the Yankee manufacturers have slain their millions of Western agriculturists." In fact, criticism of the tariff and claims of sectional loyalty were characteristic of Copperhead spokes-men and the anti-Administration press. Western realism was exemplified by the

prominent Indianapolis merchant who studied one of the wartime tariff proposals and added, "If that tax is levied, it will make me disloyal."

The institution of heavy excise duties upon distilled spirits[5] and malt liquors brought protests from distillers and farmers alike. Vallandigham and his cohorts viewed the excise tax as a blow against the West and as a war upon democratic doc-trines. Many small distillers realized that, in practice, the internal revenue program discriminated against them, and they con-sequently closed their plants. Farmers who had disposed of their surplus grain at the distilleries complained bitterly as they were forced to find other markets for their grain.

The National Bank Act of 1863 aroused some anxiety in the West, but patriotic preachments, wartime confusion, and an antipathy to wildcat banking paved the way for governmental sanction of the prin-ciples of Whiggery. Sam Medary, fired by loyalty to section and to Jacksonian con-cepts, levied a heavy editorial barrage against the "monstrous Bank Bill" and spoke the language of the Southern fire-eaters: "The West will not bleed at every pore because well-preserved and fanatical New England declares that such is her pa-triotic duty." The *Enquirer's* editor raised the spector of monopoly:

The enormity of this bill is sufficient to make General Jackson, who killed the old Bank of the United States, turn over in his coffin. . . . The design is to destroy the fixed institutions of the States, and build up a central moneyed despo-tism.

In the House of Representatives, Vallan-digham and Voorhees restated the argu-ments against monopoly and centralization

---

[5] The act of July 1, 1862 levied a tax of 20 cents per gallon upon distilled spirits. The act of March 7, 1864, increased the tax to 60 cents per gallon, and later war revenue measures raised the rate to $1.50 per gallon.

of power in the best Jacksonian and Jeffersonian tradition. Two other Midwestern Copperheads, James C. Allen and William A. Richardson, both of Illinois, led the forces which secured postponement of the taxing of the state bank notes and the granting of the "money monopoly" to the nationally chartered banks.

Those who railed at the "railroad monopoly" usually raised their voices against the "money monopoly." Frederic W. Horn, ofttimes unfairly blamed for the Wisconsin draft riots of 1862, feared "the power and influence of New England capital." M. M. Pomeroy, a La Crosse editor who developed criticism of Lincoln into an art and whose dictionary of diatribe was unabridged, believed that the war and its monetary measures made the trans-Allegheny West both "slave and servant of New England." The *See-Bote's* editor, too, contended that "the money monopoly of New England is absolutely controlling and the labor of. . . . the Western states is tributary to it." Another malcontent stated his unequivocal opposition to all banks, and criticized Hamiltonian doctrine by contending that "the doctrine of vested rights is a great humbug. . . ."

Labor, too, wore its crown of thorns. The business depression which plagued the West early in the war brought mass unemployment and labor unrest. The unemployed paraded the streets of Milwaukee, and other Midwestern cities witnessed similar scenes. A touring London *Times* correspondent observed that labor paid a heavy price in the war—that it was "ground down to the utmost extent of its power of endurance." Although opportunities for employment increased after the first year of the war, because of the withdrawal of workers into Army uniforms and the demands for war supplies, the influx of freed Negroes and border-state white refugees tended to give employers tighter control of the labor market.

The greatest resentment against emancipation came from the ranks of unskilled labor. The London *Times'* correspondent observed,

> The jealousy of the low Germans and Irish against the free negro was sufficient to set them against the war which would have brought four million of their black rivals into competition for that hard and dirty work which American freedom bestowed on them.

The *See-Bote* warned Milwaukee Germans against abolition. It headlined an editorial "Abolition the Worst Enemy of the Free White Laborer," warning its readers that employers desired abolition in order to secure "cheap labor" as it issued a call to action: "Workmen! Be Careful! Organize yourself against this element which threatens your impoverishment and annihilation." *The Crisis,* the *Chicago Times,* and the *Cincinnati Enquirer,* as leading Copperhead papers in the Midwest, repeated the same theme. Efforts of some Chicago meat-packers to employ "contraband labor" forced Irish and German workers to protest. At a public meeting they adopted the resolution that

> . . . the packing-house men of the town of South Chicago, pledge ourselves not to work for any packer, under any consideration, who will, in any manner, bring negro labor into competition with our labor.

A score of Midwestern cities suffered riots. The departure of a Cincinnati steamer, manned by an all-Negro crew, lit the fires of revolt; Cincinnati Irish attacked the Negro quarters with torches and guns. Chicago's Bridgeport Irish, the city's "unwashed Dimmycrats," staged the "Omnibus Riot" and the "Lumberdock Riot"—a tragedy in two acts. Toledo, Milwaukee, Rock Island, and Quincy workmen, among others, strongly protested the influx of cheap and competitive labor.

Laborers had other complaints, too. The $300 exemption clause in the Conscription

Act of 1863 appeared to be class legislation. Wages, until late in the war, lagged
far behind prices, which moved upward
as the Government sponsored inflation
through the issuance of greenbacks. In
spite of Republican party propaganda, the
tariff policy of the Administration levied a
heavy burden upon the millions of workers
employed in the non-protected industries.
The Contract Labor law, which permitted
employers to bring in foreign workers by
the boat-load, encouraged laborers to
strike and to organize. These dissatisfied
workmen readily justified their opposition
to the Lincoln Administration and their
presence in Copperhead ranks.

The protest of lamenting laborers and
disgruntled agrarians underwrote Midwestern Copperheadism. The malcontents,
naturally, blamed the Administration for
many of their ills. They expressed their
dissent in a variety of ways, sometimes engaging in negative measures and at times
proposing positive programs. Some agitated for compromise and peace conventions, "for union without victory"; they believed that a patched-up peace would restore their Western political balance-of-
power, regain their economic ties with the
South, and dissipate the domination of the
Northeast. The West wanted the Mississippi opened and its markets restored.
Others bid for an outlet to the sea via Canada and for direct trade with Liverpool
and London. The Illinois "Copperhead
Legislature of 1863" supported such a
measure to free Westerners from the chok-
ing grasp in which east-west trade opera-
tors held them. Most of them hid behind
the facade of state rights to protect their
democratic faith, their individual rights,
their sectional wants, and their economic
life; so they held the conscription act with
its provost-marshal system to be unconstitutional, the suspension of the writ of
habeas corpus as a move toward tyranny,

the muzzling of the press as dangerous to
life and liberty, and revitalized Whiggery
as heresy from Jeffersonian doctrine. Many
resorted to verbal and written protests and
petitions. All turned toward the polls as
the medium to redress their grievances.
The political revolt of 1862 subsequently
rocked the Republican Administration. In
the legislatures of 1863 in Illinois and Indiana, the malcontents tried to restore their
economic rights while they blended sordid
politics with mudsill machinations. Their
political blunders were a boomerang, and
Governors Yates and Morton capitalized
upon Copperhead errors of judgment and
action. In the Illinois State Constitutional
Convention of 1862 the Copperheads
spoke a Granger-like language and formu-
lated anti-railroad provisions, but the tail
of treason dragged their constitutional kite
into the ditch of defeat.

War prosperity, encouraged by Administration measures, entered the Western
scene midway in the war, and rising prices
pleased the agrarians as falling prices had
earlier displeased them. The judicious dis-
tribution of war contracts changed some
dissenters into defenders. Draft bounties
tempted some of the poor laborers and
drew them from their unhappy surroundings. Vallandigham, abstaining from tact
and illogical in tactics, gained notoriety
and stigmatized Copperheadism. Administration counter-measures and Republican
party stratagems, combined with victory at
Vicksburg, also helped to quash the
Copperhead revolt. Aroused nationalism
helped mold men's minds. But it was war
prosperity which contributed most to un-
dermining this Jeffersonian protest against
the progress of the Industrial Revolution
and its envelopment of the government. A
Cincinnati editor viewed war prosperity as
"the lance of Achilles, healing by its touch
the wounds" of death and devastation, and
the touring correspondent of the London

Times added that prosperity covered a multitude of sins. Consequently, Copperheadism collapsed and died a slow death.

Southern sectionalism had resulted in secession and had threatened the Northwest with "geographic isolation." The political and economic advance of the Northeast, on the other hand, had threatened the power of the Western sectionalists, who hid behind the tenets set forth by John Taylor of Caroline. The defeat of the South dealt a deathblow to the doctrine of secession and quashed the Jeffersonian protests of the West. Sherman's capture of Atlanta gave the lie to Copperhead charges that the war was a failure. Grant's victory at Appomatox successfully silenced those who had chanted the old refrain. "The Constitution as it is and the Union as it was." So, in the end, both the South and the West failed to stem the tide of the Industrial Revolution in America. And the new nation, maintained as one by war, prepared to enter a new era.

A fresh look at the heartland of Copperheadism, the
Northwest, is taken in the following article by JACQUE
VOEGELI (b. 1934), assistant professor of history at
Vanderbilt University and author of *Free But Not Equal,*
which extends his study of the Midwest and the Negro
through the Civil War. The author distinguishes between
antislavery sentiment and equalitarianism. He is
concerned not with the Democrats alone but with both
major parties. His view may be profitably compared with
those of Gray and Klement. What is his central thesis?
How does he explain Republican congressional policy?
How does he interpret the congressional election of 1862?
What picture does he draw of Lincoln, the political
leader?*

Jacque Voegeli

The Democrats as Racists

In a recent essay, C. Vann Woodward
wrote critically of those writers—"myth-
makers" he called them—who have created "the legend that the Mason and
Dixon Line not only divided slavery from
freedom in antebellum America," but also
"set apart racial inhumanity in the South
from benevolence, liberality and tolerance
in the North." In this "North Star Legend," the pre-Civil War North emerges as
the practicing champion of racial equality.
This myth is related to and becomes, in
fact, a part of a current interpretation of
the Civil War. In this interpretation,
which emphasizes the moral conflict,
slavery appears not primarily as a political
or emotional issue but as a thing of evil
against which men must fight. Since the
evil was sectional, the forces of good and

evil appear divided along sectional lines.
"Human dignity and freedom" as well as
"democracy" were to be restored to the
South. The North thus went to war in
1861 fighting for human dignity, freedom,
and democracy. Yet how deeply committed to human dignity and democracy
for the Negro was the North? How deeply
was it committed to equality for the
Negro?

The northern commitment to equality
cannot be measured by the amount of antislavery sentiment. Outrage over slavery
and belief in white supremacy were two
seemingly discordant strains of thought
that were often harmonized in the antislavery intellect. In the section of the country then popularly called the Northwest,
the coexistence of these two strains was

*Jacque Voegeli, "The Northwest and the Race Issue, 1861–1862," *Mississippi Valley Historical Review,* L
(September, 1963), 235–251. Most footnotes omitted.

perhaps most apparent. In that portion of the North, at any rate, humanitarian pity for the slaves did not always spring from a desire to confer equal rights on all men. Antislavery men did not necessarily understand that equality for the Negro would inexorably follow emancipation. In that section, when war broke out, opposition to the evil of slavery did not carry with it a commitment to equality for the Negro.

The Northwest comprised the seven states of Ohio, Indiana, Illinois, Michigan, Wisconsin, Minnesota, and Iowa. In 1861 it was a stronghold of white supremacy. As the nation girded for war, state constitutions and statutes reflected the racism that flourished in the region. The severity of the discriminatory legislation varied, but every state imposed legal disabilities upon its black residents. All seven states limited service in the militia to white males and barred Negroes from the suffrage. In Illinois and Indiana there were no provisions for the education of colored children, and Negroes were not recognized as competent witnesses in court trials where a white person was a party to the case. Iowa and Ohio excluded Negroes from jury service. Interracial marriages were forbidden in Michigan, Ohio, Indiana, and Illinois. Ohio denied Negroes the benefits of poor relief and provided for racially segregated public schools. Exclusion laws carrying severe penalties prohibited Negroes from settling in Indiana, Illinois, and Iowa.

Early in the war, the fate of the Negro race became a source of great concern to the Northwest. Armed conflict brought the realization that war could loosen the bonds of slavery and this in turn raised the question: What can be done with the freed slaves? This was not a new question; it had, of course, long troubled the friends of emancipation, both North and South. Now, with slavery in jeopardy for the first time, the most disturbing aspect of this problem in the Northwest was the apprehension that the freedmen would throng into the area and become social, economic, and political competitors of the whites.

Apprehension became alarm as a result of legislation of the second session of the Thirty-seventh Congress, for by the time of adjournment on July 17, 1862, Republican party members had pushed through a series of measures designed to shatter the corner-stone of the Confederacy. Both houses approved a joint resolution offering financial aid to slave states that would adopt gradual emancipation. Bondsmen in the District of Columbia and in the territories were declared free. The use of military power in returning fugitive slaves to their masters was prohibited, and a militia act liberated Union slave-soldiers and their families owned by rebels. Climaxing this program, the Confiscation Act of July 17, 1862, provided that slaves owned by persons supporting the rebellion should be forever free.[1] If enforced, this law would have freed practically every slave in the Confederacy. The congressional drive toward emancipation stirred violent partisan conflict, in and out of Congress, as Democrats and Republicans debated the consequences of freeing the slaves and plumbed the depths of the race problem. The northwestern attitude toward the Negro now received its fullest exposition.

Among the most implacable foes of emancipation were the northwestern Democrats. Although they had many constitutional and political objections to slave liberation, much of their resistance to the assault on slavery sprang from the fear that emancipation would deluge the Northwest with Negroes and challenge white suprem-

---

[1] It is not the purpose of this article to trace the course of this session of Congress, but, rather, to be concerned with the Northwest's views of the Negro, with some consideration of the influence of these attitudes on political policies.

acy there. These Democrats attacked every proposal to free the slaves or improve the lot of the free Negro. They did not defend slavery as a positive good, and they seemed ready to tolerate the institution rather than to increase the number of Negroes in the Northwest. Their attitude was that expressed by an Iowa newspaperman. He opposed "slavery *per se*"; yet he was confident that slaves would not benefit from freedom and that there was "little doubt of the demoralizing effect it will have upon the white race in the North . . . to have these emancipated blacks introduced among them." Representative Samuel S. Cox of Ohio observed, "If slavery is bad, the condition of . . . Ohio, with an unrestrained black population, only double what we now have partly subservient, partly slothful, partly criminal, and all disadvantageous and ruinous, will be far worse."[2]

Skillfully exploiting the dread of a Negro invasion of the Northwest, Democrats protested that slave confiscation and emancipation would send the freed slaves surging into the Northwest, and that ruin and degradation would follow in their wake. They argued, in part, from reasons of economic interest. The withdrawal of the southern laboring force would destroy the prosperity of the South, thereby depriving the Northwest of its market for surplus goods. Bills calling for federal compensation to slave states which would adopt emancipation were scored as projects for taxing the whites to build black communities in the North. Negro immigrants, they said, would drain the northern economy because they were thieves and chronic paupers. Wage earners were

warned that hordes of unskilled competitors would inundate the Northwest to degrade society, reduce wages, and drive the whites from their jobs.

Professing to believe that the Republicans intended to "equalize" the races, Democrats assailed the specter of racial equality with an appeal to white superiority. Because the Negro was inherently inferior, said the Democrats, equality for the black man would contaminate northwestern society and politics and debase the American people. A Republican bill authorizing the exchange of diplomatic representatives with Haiti and Liberia drew a stream of abuse from alarmed Democrats who suspected that this was an instrument for forcing equality. Representative Cox objected to receiving colored diplomats in Washington, he said, because history taught that "these Commonwealths and this Union were made for white men; that this Government is a Government of white men; that the men who made it never intended by anything they did to place the black race upon an equality with the white." To Representative William A. Richardson of Illinois, the Republicans were mocking the Almighty: "God made the white man superior to the black, and no legislation will undo or change the decrees of Heaven . . . and unlike the abolition equalizationists I find no fault and utter no complaint against the wisdom of our Creator."

While the Democrats protested emancipation and vilified the Negro, Republicans slowly pushed their antislavery program through Congress. When Congress convened in December, 1861, there was no consensus on slavery within the Republican party. A deep gulf separated those abolitionists who interpreted the war as a divine command to destroy slavery from the moderate and conservative men, most of whom advanced haltingly to the position

[2]In 1860 the number and percentage of Negroes in each state were as follows: Illinois, 7,628 (0.4); Indiana, 11,428 (0.9); Ohio, 36,673 (1.3); Wisconsin, 1,171 (0.2); Minnesota, 259 (0.1); Michigan, 6,799 (0.9); and Iowa, 333 (0.2).

that the confiscation of slaves could sap the strength of the rebels. Emancipationists from the Northwest presented an appealing case for confiscating Confederate slaves. Confiscation and emancipation, they maintained, would cripple or crush the southern war effort, save the Union, insure future national unity, and punish the South. Seldom, however, was the plight of the enslaved given as the chief justification for emancipation.

Many considerations determined this approach to the slavery problem. To most Republican congressmen in 1862 the war was being waged for the restoration of the Union, with or without slavery. Besides this, sound political tactics demanded that "Union," not "abolition," be the cry to unify the North. The party in power was especially sensitive to Democratic accusations that rabid abolitionists had caused the South to secede, seized control of the Republican party, and were forcing unconstitutional abolition measures upon Congress. The plea that slave liberation was the price of military victory was partially designed to overcome the constitutional scruples of those strict constructionists who doubted the constitutionality of the slave confiscation proposals. There was still another reason for not converting the war into an avowed abolition crusade: Republicans of every persuasion knew that the Northwest would not shed blood solely in behalf of a race it despised. Excessive emphasis upon the humanitarian objectives of emancipation would have lent truth to the Democratic complaint that the Republicans were fighting a war to free the Negro. Consequently, although they denounced slavery as a crime against God, humanity, morality, and natural rights, northwestern Republicans made it clear that they were primarily concerned with restoring the Union.

The Democratic outcry that emancipation would inundate the Northwest with Negroes gravely disturbed the Republicans, for they knew of the deep-seated opposition in the Northwest to the entry of colored persons. Republican members of Congress warned of this feeling. When Senator Jacob M. Howard of Michigan was told by a colleague that if the slaves were freed and distributed among the various states in proportion to the white population, Michigan would have about 123,000 blacks instead of the 6,800 it then had, Howard retorted, "Canada is very near us, and affords a fine market for 'wool.'" Senator Lyman Trumbull of Illinois candidly told the Senate, "There is a very great aversion in the West—I know it to be so in my state—against having free negroes come among us. Our people want nothing to do with the negro." Time and time again Republicans voiced these sentiments. Some party leaders arraigned the section for its hostility toward Negroes, but no one questioned the prevalence or intensity of this feeling.

This Negrophobia impeded and imperiled the passage of slave confiscation and emancipation measures in 1862. Senator Trumbull, who was himself the chief draftsman of the confiscation bill, discerned that hostility to Negroes posed one of the most potent objections to his proposal. The people of the Northwest, Trumbull said, were asking the supporters of confiscation: "'What will you do with them [slaves]; we do not want them set free to come in among us; we know it is wrong that the rebels should have the benefit of their services to fight us; but what do you propose to do with them?'" An Ohio congressman put it more bluntly. Incensed by the slow progress of confiscation proposals, he cried: "The nation has been led astray quite long enough by the miserable partisan war cry that emancipation means 'to turn the niggers loose.' "

To overcome these objections, a number of Republican leaders—both radicals and conservatives—brought forth a theory destined to become a Republican panacea for all the ills of emancipation. According to this theory, slave liberation would not only remove slavery from the South but would take the Negro from the Northwest. It was slavery, both the Republican press and politicians emphasized, that caused the flight of blacks from the cotton kingdom. Free the slaves, they said, and a warm climate, abundant land, a demand for their labor, a sentimental attachment to the South, and northern race prejudice would induce the freedmen to stay on southern soil. Furthermore, the same forces would send northern Negroes rushing southward. Republicans from the middle states joined their northwestern brethren in this refrain. Two sanguine emancipationists, George W. Julian of Indiana and Albert G. Riddle of Ohio, expected freedom in the South to drain both the North and Canada of their colored residents.

To what extent these Republicans actually believed that northern Negroes would go South to freedom is difficult to ascertain. But such pronouncements were certainly more than Machiavellian utterances fashioned to deceive the people of the North. The idea that the Negro was a creature of the tropics was a part of the stereotype of the black race. In private correspondence as well as in public statements, antislavery men declared their belief that slavery alone prevented northern Negroes from moving to the South. David Noggle, a Wisconsin judge who boasted of his radicalism, censured Senator James R. Doolittle for espousing the colonization of the slaves. "With all due deference to your wild notions of colonization," he wrote, "I think you can't but believe that [by] abol-

ishing Slavery in the Southern States the Northern States would be speedily cleared of their present free colored population." This same belief led Secretary of the Treasury Salmon P. Chase of Ohio to advocate military emancipation in the Deep South. In a letter to Major General Benjamin F. Butler, then the Union Commander of the Department of the Gulf, Chase wrote that "many honest men really think they [Negroes] are not to be permitted to reside permanently in the Northern States." While he said he had no objection to the presence of colored people in his state, Chase felt that they would prefer the southern climate. "Let, therefore, the South be opened to negro emigration by emancipation along the Gulf, and it is easy to see that the blacks of the North will slide southward, and leave behind them no question to quarrel about as far as they are concerned."

Although many Republicans expressed such views, the party adhered officially to colonization as the answer to the problems which would be created by emancipation. The slaves that were to be freed were to be colonized in foreign lands. In the vanguard of the deportation movement were prominent northwestern Republicans—President Abraham Lincoln, Senators John Sherman of Ohio, James R. Doolittle of Wisconsin, Trumbull and Orville H. Browning of Illinois, and Henry S. Lane of Indiana.

These men were convinced that physical differences between the races created racial antagonism that would not be dispelled by emancipation. Senator Doolittle, a chief advocate of colonization, wrote that "the question of race is a more troublesome one than the question of condition." The colonizationists urged—since history and evidence on every hand indicated that white Americans would not admit black men to the equality to which all men aspired—that emancipation be followed by removal of the freedman from the United States. Such a course would benefit both races. The whites would profit from the departure of an alien race, and the blacks would escape from domination and oppression. The most concise statement of the philosophy of colonization came from President Lincoln. On August 14, 1862, shortly after Congress adjourned, Lincoln addressed a deputation of colored men and pointed out that both humanitarianism and racial antipathy nourished the colonization movement. Lincoln stated that the broad physical difference between the two races was disadvantageous to both. "I think your race suffer very greatly, many of them by living among us," he said, "while ours suffer from your presence. . . . If this is admitted, it affords a reason at least why we should be separated." He reminded his audience that freedom did not bring equality to the Negro; for "on this broad continent, not a single man of your race is made the equal of a single man of ours."

Similar pleas for deportation were advanced by Republican congressmen from the Northwest. They emphasized the point that as long as the Negro race resided in the United States, it was doomed to subordination and ostracism. In bestowing freedom upon a proscribed people, the nation was obligated to resettle the outcasts in foreign lands where they could enjoy equal rights and govern themselves. Many congressmen, especially those from New England, protested that colonization was inhumane, impractical, uneconomic, and un-Christian. With the strong support of the Northwest and the middle states, Congress overrode these objections. It incorporated into both the confiscation act and the District of Columbia emancipation act provisions for colonizing those slaves,

liberated by that legislation, who were willing to leave the United States.[3]

There were also stern political exigencies that turned the Republican party to colonization in 1862. Some Republican strategists, including Lincoln, hoped that the adoption of deportation would persuade the loyal slave states to move toward emancipation. But it was the political situation in the North that insured Republican support for colonization. In the Northwest, Pennsylvania, and New Jersey, insistent voices clamored for positive action to shield the North from a Negro invasion. Colonization became a key part of the program to make slave confiscation and emancipation more palatable to the free states. Deportation would blunt the threat of a Negro ingress and thus would relieve emancipation of a dreaded burden.

Republicans, in fact, openly avowed that deportation was designed to keep the freedmen out of the North. When Senator Trumbull placed a confiscation measure before the Senate, he said that the colonization proposal in the bill would answer those northwesterners who wanted the slaves freed but objected to having them brought into their section. Republican Senator John C. Ten Eyck of New Jersey, a member of the committee which considered the confiscation bill, announced that the committee thought the colonization section to be "of the utmost importance." He contended that the North's opposition to an influx of Negroes called for a declaration of the government's policy on colonization. After Congress had passed the acts containing provisions for voluntary colonization, Assistant Secretary of the Interior John P. Usher of Indiana pressed President Lincoln to accept a plan for colo-

---

[3]In a key vote in the Senate, Republicans from the Northwest, New York, Pennsylvania, and New Jersey voted thirteen to three for colonization while New England senators voted against it, six to five.

nizing the freedmen in Chiriqui. On August 2, 1862, Usher advised the President that such action would allay apprehensions that the North was going to be overrun by free Negroes. Twelve days later, at his widely publicized conference with the colored men, the President noted that hopes for freedom would be greatly enhanced if some free Negroes would accept colonization. "There is an unwillingness on the part of our people, harsh as it may be, for you free colored people to remain with us," he said. "Now, if you could give a start to the white people, you would open a wide door for many to be made free."[4]

Throughout the congressional discussion of colonization and other measures relating to the condition of the Negro, it was apparent that northwestern Republicans were not advocating racial equality. If any of them were egalitarians, they pondered their principles in silence. They had joined with other Republicans in enacting legislation intended to improve the lot of the black man, particularly in the District of Columbia. They were, in this respect, considerate of the humanity of the black man; but at the same time they disclaimed any goal of racial equality. They agreed that political and social rights were outside the province of federal law; only the states could confer political privileges, and each individual could regulate his own social relations. Charity and humanity, not equality, were their watchwords. Sympathy for the victims of slavery, a spirit of *noblesse oblige*, and an urge to do justice to the oppressed inspired their benevolence. Representative John Hutchins of Ohio said: "These measures have no relation to political or social equality. . . . Because we are willing to do justice to the humblest in society, does it follow that we are bound to

extend to them the same social and political privileges which we enjoy?" To Senator James Harlan, an Iowa Republican, civilized society was obligated to protect the Negroes, "another feeble people," but their freedom would neither bring nor require equality with the whites.

Meanwhile, Republicans at home in the Northwest displayed much the same attitude. Although the Ohio state legislature Republicans withstood the demand for Negro-exclusion legislation, discriminatory laws continued to prevail. Republican-dominated legislatures in Iowa and Ohio met and adjourned without altering the anti-Negro laws on their statute books. The heavily Republican Iowa legislature amended its militia law, but continued to limit the enrollment to white males.

There were some northwesterners who wished to grant equal political rights to the Negro. The referendum on a new state constitution for Illinois indicated the size of this minority in that state. In a direct vote on the franchise, the people of Illinois, by a majority of over five to one, chose to continue its ban on Negro suffrage and office holding. In such an atmosphere, no political party and few, if any, politicians could admit egalitarian principles and survive.

As they talked at home and in Congress, many northwestern Republican stalwarts spoke the language of white supremacy. Governor William Dennison, a founder of the Republican party in Ohio, referred to the "superior [white] race." Because of the Negro's "kindly and affectionate" nature, remarked the Chicago *Tribune*, he is "rarely agitated by the profound passions which belong to his superiors." Republican Senators Sherman, Browning, Doolittle, and Harlan were certain that a higher law transcended man-made rules and governed race relations. They stressed that natural instincts implanted by the Creator forbade equality of the races. God and na-

---

[4] The timing of this interview seems to indicate that Lincoln publicly reaffirmed his faith in colonization at this time to allay northern fears of a Negro influx.

ture, not prejudice, accounted for racial antipathy, and what God had decreed they did not propose to deny. The law of caste, asserted Sherman, was the unchangeable "law of God. . . . The whites and the blacks will always be separate, or where they are brought together, one will be inferior to the other." According to Browning and Doolittle, human instincts caused white resistance to social and political equality. Doolittle stated that "in the temperate zone, the Caucausian race has always been dominant, and always will be. In the torrid zone the colored man dominates and will forever. . . . The Creator has written it upon the earth and upon the race." Responding to a query about the possibility of interracial marriages, Senator Harlan asked, "Has the hand of nature fixed no barrier to such loathsome associations?"

Events in the summer of 1862 warned of intensifying hostility toward the black race. In a June referendum on a new state constitution, Illinois voters refused to ratify the proposed constitution, but they overwhelmingly approved an article that prohibited Negroes from settling in the state and denied suffrage and public office to Negroes and mulattoes. Voting on these two provisions separately, the people endorsed the exclusion section by a vote of 171,896 to 71,806. Since the defeat of the constitution, reputedly a Democratic party document, was hailed as a Republican victory, the vote for the anti-Negro article was obviously drawn from both parties. Later that summer anti-Negro sentiment became even more apparent, when in July and August serious race riots flared in New Albany (Indiana), Chicago, Toledo, and Cincinnati.

The campaign which began in the summer of 1862 for the fall congressional elections found both emancipation and the status of the Negro as major political issues in the Northwest. Militant Democratic state conventions drafted caustic resolutions condemning emancipation as an unconstitutional, impractical measure that portended ruin for the region. The Iowa Democrats resolved that "this is a Government of white men, and was established exclusively for the white race; that the negroes are not entitled to, and ought not to be admitted to political or social equality with the white race." To halt economic competition between the races, the Democrats of Ohio opposed emancipation and demanded a ban on Negro immigration into the Buckeye State. Excoriating slave liberation, the Illinois and Indiana Democratic conventions demanded enforcement of their exclusion laws on the grounds that white men alone were suited to the free institutions of their states. Wisconsin Democrats adopted and published an address which asserted that social equality of the races was contrary to the laws of nature: "Nature never placed the races together; when brought together the servitude of the inferior is the best condition for both races."

Standing upon these party platforms, Democratic candidates and newspapers fired their familiar barrage of social, political, and economic objections at emancipation. If the slaves were liberated, they would fly to the North where their contact with a superior race would degrade white society, their economic rivalry would reduce wages, and their political competition would contaminate politics. Democrats spied the spirit of "equalization" lurking within every scheme of the Republicans. The preliminary proclamation of emancipation, issued by Lincoln on September 22, 1862, served as a prime target for the Democrats. In order to preserve white supremacy and repel the black invaders, the Democrats argued, the Republican party should be turned out of power before the President could execute his emancipation proclamation.[5]

On the emancipation and Negro issues, the campaign strategy of the Republican and Union party organizations in the Northwest usually followed a well-established line: slave confiscation and emancipation were desperately needed to win the war and restore the Union. Humanitarian goals were generally shunted aside while the voters were reassured that Union, not abolition, was the object of the war. On one point the Republicans concurred with the Democrats—Negroes were not wanted in the Northwest. Instead of extending an invitation to the slaves to seek their freedom in the free states, they made it clear that they neither desired nor expected any increase in the colored population of the area. From the press, pulpit, and political rostrum radicals and conservatives sounded the familiar cliché: slavery was driving southern Negroes into the Northwest, but emancipation in the Confederate states would hold the freedmen in the land of their labor and lure northern Negroes to the congenial South. Colonization, too, was proffered as a means of reducing the Negro population. Democratic charges of Republican egalitarianism were either ignored or dismissed as malicious slander. Irritated by the allegation that Republican policies would lead to equality of the races and that "our volunteers are periling their lives to make niggers the equal of whites," the Indianapolis *Journal* exclaimed, "what a monstrous and villainous lie."

In the elections of October and November, 1862, the Democrats swept to victory in the Northwest. They carried Ohio, Illinois, and Indiana, and registered impressive gains in Michigan and Wisconsin. For the federal House of Representatives, the Democrats elected fourteen out of nineteen members from Ohio, seven of eleven in Indiana, nine of fourteen in Illinois, and divided six Wisconsin seats with their rivals. The next Congress would contain thirty-four Democrats out of a total of sixty-four northwestern representatives, a gain of eighteen seats for the resurgent party.

Many factors inspired the political revolt against the party of Lincoln in the 1862 elections. In the Northwest, arbitrary arrests by federal authorities, suspension of the habeas corpus privilege, the emancipation proclamation, and a disappointing military situation plagued the nominees of the Republican and Union parties. The emancipation issue with its many ramifications played a leading role in the Democratic victory. Many northwestern Republicans conceded its impact. Senator Browning informed Lincoln that the proclamation suspending the writ of habeas corpus and the emancipation edict had defeated the party. John Sherman wrote that the "ill timed proclamation contributed to the general result." According to Unionist Thomas Ewig, a former United States senator, Lincoln had ruined the Union party in Ohio by issuing the proclamations. A clarion of radical Republicanism, the Cleveland *Leader*, asserted that Ohio and Illinois had voted against emancipation.

This opposition to emancipation was primarily the product of Negrophobia aggravated by the threat of a massive influx of Negroes. H. S. Bundy, an unsuccessful Union party aspirant for Congress from Ohio, wrote Salmon P. Chase that the emancipation proclamation had been delivered just in time to defeat him and many other Union candidates in the Indiana and Ohio elections. "I had thought until this year the cry of 'nigger' & 'abolitionism,' were played out but they never

---

[5]A number of Republican and Unionist newspaper editors contented themselves with the observation that the emancipation proclamation was a "war measure" and then ignored it until after the elections. But the majority followed the course indicated above.

had as much power & effect in this part of the state as at the recent elections." The disgruntled Chicago *Tribune* interpreted the political reverses as a signal for the Republican party to re-emphasize its devotion to the "white race." It counseled fellow Republicans to justify the emancipation proclamation in terms of its effect upon "the happiness, the freedom and the prosperity of the white men of the North. . . . We need not go beyond that; if we do we bring the prejudices of caste and races into full play, and by weakening the efforts of the North, impair the good the proclamation promises."

Elated Democrats hailed the elections of 1862 as a repudiation of the emancipation heresy. To the Democratic Columbus *Crisis* the elections, a contest of *"black vs. white,"* had resolved that Ohio would never become the refuge for southern Negroes. Representative Cox said the victory of his party had brought forth a new commandment, "Thou shalt not degrade the white race by such intermixtures as emancipation would bring." "The people," an Illinois Democrat told the House of Representatives, "are sick and tired of this eternal talk upon the Negro, and they have expressed their disgust unmistakably in the recent elections."

Impressed by the North's persistent hostility toward the free Negro, President Lincoln strove to assuage the fears of the people. In his annual message to Congress in December, 1862, he contended that liberation and deportation of the slaves would benefit northern white men. He strongly recommended the adoption of a constitutional amendment calling for compensated emancipation and voluntary colonization of the freedmen. The claim that liberated Negroes would displace white labor the President termed "largely imaginary, if not sometimes malicious." If the freedmen should remain where they were, "they jostle no white laborers; if they leave their old places, they leave them open to white laborers." Emancipation alone would probably improve the wages of whites, and the deportation of colored workers would certainly increase the earnings of white men.

The President then turned to the fear "that the freed people will swarm forth, and cover the whole land":

Equally distributed among the whites of the whole country . . . there would be but one colored to seven whites. Could the one, in any way, greatly disturb the seven? . . . But why should emancipation south, send the free people north? People, of any color, seldom run, unless there be something to run from. *Heretofore* colored people, to some extent, have fled north from bondage; and *now*, perhaps, from both bondage and destitution. But if gradual emancipation and deportation be adopted, they will have neither to flee from. Their old masters will give them wages . . . till new homes can be found for them in congenial climes, and with people of their own blood and race. . . . And, in any event, cannot the north decide for itself, whether to receive them?

Under the skillful pen of Lincoln, emancipation, colonization, and exclusion became deterrents to a Negro invasion of the North.

By the end of 1862, the Northwest had amply demonstrated that ultimate equality for the Negro had not been a war aim when the conflict began. The concept of the innate superiority of the "white race" cut across party lines and pervaded the mind of the Northwest. Moral opposition to slavery helped kindle the "irrepressible conflict," but moral principle had not abated the Northwest's determination to preserve white supremacy.

Democrats in both houses of the Thirty-seventh Congress come under scruntiny in this careful study. LEONARD P. CURRY (b. 1929), associate professor of history at the University of Louisville, addresses himself to the questions of the opposition members' loyalty to the Union, their support of the war effort, responsibility in their attitude toward nonwar legislation, the degree of party unity, and the Democrats' place in the spectrum of political philosophy. Curry bases his analysis on voting performance. Note the degree of Democratic cooperation with Republicans and the degree of disagreement between House and Senate Republicans. Curry's *Blueprint for Modern America: Nonmilitary Legislation of the First Civil War Congress* (1968) amplifies this essay.*

Leonard P. Curry

The Democrats as the Loyal Opposition

The Civil War is all too frequently viewed as a Republican war (on the part of the Union) against the Democratic Confederacy, and when Democrats are mentioned in relation to the wartime experiences of the Union it is generally to equate the Democratic party with Copperheadism. All of which is an accurate reflection of Republican propaganda but bears little resemblance to reality. For the Democratic party (unlike the Republican party) was not a sectional one and its northern wing (which the Charleston convention demonstrated to be the majority) was still a force to be reckoned with. In the nonseceding states the Republicans had managed to capture only 48.8 per cent of the popular vote in the presidential elec-

tion of 1860 and had outpolled the Democrats by only 150,000 votes. In seven of the twenty-two Union states participating in this election, the Republicans had failed to obtain majorities, and in two others (Indiana and Illinois) their vote amounted to about 51 percent of the total. Further, Republican control of other important Union states was by no means firm, as the political events of the first years of the Civil War demonstrated. By 1863 the Democrats had elected governors in New York and New Jersey and senators from Illinois, Indiana, and Pennsylvania. In addition, the convening of the Thirty-eighth Congress in 1863 found the Democrats in solid control of the House delegations from Illinois, Indiana, New York, and Ohio, while

*Leonard P. Curry, "Congressional Democrats, 1861–1863," *Civil War History,* XII (September, 1966), 213–229. Some footnotes omitted.

the Pennsylvania and Wisconsin delegations were equally divided between the Democrats and "Unionists." And even in the Thirty-seventh Congress the Republicans held only 106 House seats, eight fewer than in the previous Congress.

The Democrats most assuredly cannot be dismissed as politically inconsequential during the early Civil War period. This paper is designed to explore one aspect of the national political process during these years—Democratic actions in the Thirty-seventh Congress (1861–1863).

It must be said at the outset that there was never any question of the Democrats challenging Republican control of both houses of Congress. The House of Representatives eventually consisted of 181 seats and, of these, only forty-nine were ever held by the Democrats (though fifty-five Democratic representatives served in the House at one time or another during this Congress). A contest for the Speakership did, in fact, develop, but it was a struggle within the Republican party in which the Democrats did not involve themselves. By July, 1861, there were only fourteen Democratic senators and, consequently, any challenge to the Republicans in the upper house would have been equally futile. Further, though its political potential remained impressive, the Democratic party had lost a sizable block of its legislative leadership when the seats of the southern senators and representatives were vacated. In the preceding Congress the eleven states of the new Confederacy had been represented by twenty-two Democratic senators and (in addition to some "South Americans") fifty Democratic representatives. Of these, only seventeen representatives and four senators had not been members of the previous Congress and many had a great deal of seniority and prestige. There can be little doubt that the congressional Demo-

crats were severely weakened by these losses.

The Senate, more than the House, had been the center of prewar Democratic congressional power and leadership. In this body the party suffered further losses. Death removed Stephen A. Douglas of Illinois, John R. Thomson of New Jersey, and James A. Pearce of Maryland. John C. Breckinridge of Kentucky and the two Missouri senators, Waldo P. Johnson and Trusten Polk, left their seats to accept Confederate military commissions. Jesse D. Bright of Indiana was expelled in February, 1862, on a charge of disloyalty, and Andrew Johnson left the Senate shortly thereafter to become military governor of Tennessee.

Serving throughout the entire life of the Thirty-seventh Congress were James A. Bayard and Willard Saulsbury of Delaware, James A. McDougall and Milton S. Latham of California, Henry M. Rice of Minnesota, Lazarus Powell of Kentucky, and James W. Nesmith of Oregon. They were joined at various times during this Congress by John B. Henderson of Missouri, Benjamin Stark of Oregon, William A. Richardson of Illinois, David Turpie of Indiana, and James W. Wall of New Jersey. For various reasons, none of these senators either assumed or was conceded a position of leadership and the Senate Democrats remained unorganized.

In all, nineteen Democrats sat in the Senate of the United States during the three sessions of the Thirty-seventh Congress, but total Democratic strength in that body ranged from ten to fourteen. During the short special session in July and August, 1861, the number was fourteen; throughout most of the second and third sessions the figure was eleven. This was admittedly a small number compared to the thirty to thirty-two Republicans who sat in the upper house.[1] But one peculiar aspect of the situation should not be overlooked. The Republican majority, consistently denying the validity of secession, insisted that the Senate still consisted of sixty-eight members. Thus, thirty-five votes constituted a quorum, and at no time did the Republican membership reach this figure. It is obvious, therefore, that had the Democrats chosen to abstain, it would have been exceedingly difficult for the Senate to have mustered a quorum. This circumstance may help to explain the fact that the Senate consistently took a less advanced position on issues involving slavery and confiscation than did the House, which was not inhibited by such strict legalisms.

But it must also be pointed out that the Democrats made no real effort to thwart the majority will. Democratic absenteeism was high; on twenty-seven of the ninety-six votes examined, a majority of the Democratic senators failed to vote.[2] In well over half the instances, however, 60 per cent or more were present and voting. It must also be remembered that many of these absences were unavoidable. Pearce, Thomson, and Rice were seriously ill during the latter part of the long second session, when many important measures were brought to a vote. William P. Fessenden of Maine, the Senate Republican leader, specifically acknowledged the good faith demonstrated by the Democrats, when, on July 29, 1861, he castigated the members of his own party for abandoning the Senate floor. "I have no sort of complaint to make of the gentlemen of the Opposition," he said.

"They have given us a large proportion of their votes, and ordinarily attend as long as we could expect them to attend, to aid us to get through with the business; and it has been so from the beginning of this session."

It is easy to document both of Fessenden's assertions. On more than 90 per cent of the Senate votes examined, the withdrawal of the Democrats would have left the Senate without a quorum. That the members of the minority did not abstain is, at least to some extent, a measure of the responsible nature of the Democratic opposition in the Senate.[3] It can be argued that any such action would have provoked the Republicans to modify their policy on the nature of a quorum. But such a change would have been exceedingly difficult to accomplish, for once the policy was established, only a vote of the Senate could overturn it. This, in turn, would have required the presence of a quorum (under the old policy), which would have been impossible to obtain without the cooperation of the Democrats and Unionists. There were other barriers as well. In May, 1862, Republican John Sherman of Ohio, anticipating increasing difficulty in obtaining a quorum as the second session wore on, introduced a resolution declaring a quorum to consist of a majority of the senators elected and entitled to seats. The Committee on the Judiciary, however, recommended the indefinite postponement of the resolution; the Senate itself went even further, tabling it by a vote of nineteen to eighteen. On this vote eight Republicans joined with the six Unionists and five Democrats voting to shelve the measure. These majority senators were mostly repre-

---

[1] In addition, three senators during the first session, six during the second, and seven during the third can be classified as Unionists.

[2] All subsequent observations on the voting performance of individual Democratic senators and of the Senate Democrats as a body are based on an analysis of this ninety-six vote sample.

[3] For the purposes of this paper the terms "Democrats" and "the minority" are used interchangeably. Hence, the minority party or bloc referred to does not include Unionists unless this fact is specifically stated.

sentatives of the Conservative faction of the Republican Party (e.g., Orville H. Browning and Edgar Cowan). It seems clear that, all considerations of ideological consistency aside, the Conservative Republican senators were by no means anxious for the minority to be deprived of its ultimate parliamentary weapon, the threatened use of which could facilitate Conservative attempts to modify Radical emancipation and confiscation proposals.

There is one additional aspect of the quorum question to be considered. It seems doubtful that a Senate resolution could have accomplished what Sherman wanted. Indeed, Vice President Hannibal Hamlin might have considered such a resolution binding, but Hamlin was often absent. President Pro Tempore Solomon Foot of Vermont took occasion twice during the debates on the quorum resolution to cite precedents and advance arguments against the proposed change. While he did not directly state that he would ignore the resolution, if passed, his remarks strongly suggest that this was his intention. Such action would have created a chaotic situation, and the desire to avoid an open party split may have been the consideration which eventually moved a few Moderate and Radical Republicans to join their Conservative colleagues in support of the tabling motion.

The Democratic senators not only did not resort to the use of legislative blackmail based on the quorum ruling, they also avoided fractious opposition on almost all measures, thus meriting the additional commendation contained in Fessenden's statement: "They have given us a large proportion of their votes." It should first be noted that civil and military appropriations bills were usually passed by the Senate without a division and with very little discussion. Measures providing for in-creases in the army and navy and the re-organization of those services were normally passed under the same conditions, provided there was no attempt made by the Republicans to insert provisions for arming Negroes or confirming earlier presidential acts. Such debate as did take place was conducted almost exclusively by the majority members and, in short, there was (with the exceptions noted above) practically no Democratic opposition to the passage of these war measures.

While this performance of the minority senators accords poorly with the "Copperhead" image of Civil War Democrats, it is, though commendable, scarcely remarkable. And it hardly requires a dramatic re-evaluation of the role of the Democratic Party by any of the numerous scholars who long ago rejected the partisan canards of the era of rebellion and reunion. What is more surprising, however, is the Democratic stand on non-war legislation. The ninety-six votes analyzed for the purpose of this study include twenty-seven involving slavery and the Negro, eleven dealing with financial legislation, ten concerned with various aspects of confiscation legislation, eight involving the confirmation of presidential acts of doubtful legality, and seven dealing with public land and public improvement measures (e.g., the Homestead Act, the Land Grant College Act, and the Pacific Railway Act). These issues certainly were not directly connected with the war effort, and they were, moreover, peculiarly those which might be expected to move the Democrats to vigorous opposition and to divide the Senate along party lines. Such an assumption is difficult to sustain. On more than 55 per cent of the votes involving slavery and the Negro, a majority of the Democratic senators formed a part of the over-all Senate majority, and in almost a quarter of the cases a majority of the Democrats voted with the Republican majority.[4] Democratic voting on the other issues listed is equally revealing. The Democratic majority formed a part of the Senate majority on more than 35 per cent of the financial votes, 50 per cent of the votes involving confiscation, 50 per cent of the presidential indemnification votes, and more than 70 per cent of the votes dealing with public lands and public improvements. Democratic and Republican majorities were allied on more than a quarter of the votes involving finances, 40 per cent of those dealing with confiscation,[5] and almost 43 per cent of the public land and public improvement votes.[6] Even in an area as sensitive and notoriously partisan as Senate membership the Democratic majority constituted a part of the Senate majority almost 43 per cent of the time and joined with the Republican majority in almost 15 per cent of the cases. The entire ninety-six-vote sample illustrates that the Democratic majority formed a part of the Senate majority more than 53 per cent of the time,[7] and joined with the Republican majority on more than 27 per cent of the votes.[8]

The Democratic Senate opposition was assuredly not fractious and, indeed, was frequently not truly opposition. In fact, the Democrats had better records than the Republicans in support of several "Republican" measures. The Land Grant College Act was passed by a majority including 83.3 per cent of the Democrats and 82.1 per cent of the Republicans.[9] On several procedural and amendatory votes on the Pacific Railway Bill the Democratic senators were demonstrably more friendly to the measure than the Republicans. On May 13, 1862, all of the Democrats and just over 30 per cent of the Republicans favored making the bill a special order.[10] On May 21, 1862, a motion to take up the Pacific Railway Bill was carried by a majority which included all the Democrats and less than 40 per cent of the Republicans.[11] On June 13 and June 20, 1862, two crippling amendments were defeated by majorities containing, respectively, 100 per cent and slightly over 85 per cent of the Democrats. On these same votes the Republican percentages were 32 and 50. Furthermore, 80 per cent of the Democrats and just over 60 per cent of the Republicans supported the establishment of the Department of Agriculture. And on February 14, 1862, all of the Democrats and slightly less than 83 per cent of the Republicans combined to table a resolution which, in essence, censured Secretary of the Navy Welles.

On other measures, though Republican support exceeded that given by the Democrats, the contributions of the minority were not inconsiderable. More than 57 per cent of the Democrats voted for the Legal Tender Bill; more than 85 per cent supported the January, 1862, pledge to levy

---

[4] Included are one vote on which there was no Democratic majority, one vote on which there was no Republican majority, and one vote on which there was no Senate majority.

[5] Included are two votes on which the Republicans were evenly divided.

[6] Included is one vote on which there was no Republican majority.

[7] Included are three votes on which there was no Senate majority and two votes on which the Democrats were evenly divided. In just over half the cases the Democratic vote was unanimous.

[8] Included are four votes on which the Republicans were evenly divided and two votes on which there was no Democratic majority.

[9] The percentages given here and on subsequent votes are the percentages of the party members present and voting.

[10] The motion failed by a vote of seventeen to nineteen.

[11] The vote on the motion was twenty-three to sixteen.

taxes which would yield $150,000,000 annually; and more than 85 per cent voted for the Pacific Railway Bill (the Republican percentage was slightly higher, for it was not politically feasible for most Republicans to vote directly against the measure). Fifty per cent of the minority party voted to authorize the President to seize and operate railways and telegraph lines, and almost 55 per cent supported even so grossly partisan a measure as the Nevada Statehood Bill. These figures clearly indicate that Fessenden's assessment of Democratic operations proved eminently correct.

It was not to be expected that in a Senate overwhelmingly Republican the Democratic member should be very active in sponsoring legislation. For this role they had little inclination and less opportunity. Yet even here the minority made some contributions. Senator McDougall headed the select committee on the Pacific Railway Bill and had charge of that measure during the entire period that it was before the Senate. In addition, he was the leader in agitating the measure on the floor before it reached the upper house. Pearce, the ranking Democratic member of the Committee on Finance, took charge of a miscellaneous appropriations bill at a critical juncture and was largely responsible for the elimination of a provision which, in effect, censured Secretary of the Treasury Chase for his role in the negotiation of the treasury note printing contract And other measures of minor importance were sponsored by Bayard, Nesmith, and McDougall.

Should all of the foregoing be taken to mean that the Senate Democrats had consciously or unconsciously abandoned all hope of unity among themselves or opposition to the majority? Hardly. There was,

indeed, a high degree of unity exhibited by the Democratic senators on the votes analyzed. This unity is, perhaps, all the more remarkable when it is remembered that the party had been deeply divided in the 1860 election (among the senators, however, only McDougall, Nesmith, Henderson, and Richardson had supported Douglas). It might be noted, additionally, that the Democrats had had no experience with minority operations in the Senate for fifteen years; were a more decided minority than any major party since the Era of Good Feelings; experienced numerous membership shifts during this Congress; and had lost many of their erstwhile legislative leaders. Of the chairmen of major committees in the Thirty-sixth Congress, only Bayard (Judiciary) was a member of the Thirty-seventh. Further, the other Democrats who had held minor committee chairmanships in the Thirty-sixth Congress (Bright, Andrew Johnson, Pearce, and Thomson) either died or resigned or were expelled before the end of 1862.

Democratic Senate unity was, apparently, not achieved by institutional means—there was certainly no acknowledged leader of the Senate minority nor, from all evidence, were any official caucuses held. That this unity existed, however, is undeniable. In almost 45 per cent of the roll calls analyzed the Democrats cast unanimous votes, and in almost 70 per cent of the votes 80 per cent or more of the minority senators were united. It might be noted, for purposes of comparison, that on these same roll calls the Republicans cast unanimous votes just under 16 per cent of the time, and in slightly fewer than 40 per cent of the cases did 80 per cent or more of the majority senators combine. Democratic unity fell below 60 per cent in only 8.3 per cent of the cases. By contrast, less than 60 per cent of the Republicans voted together more than a quarter of the time.

All the Democrats except Andrew Johnson, who was a law unto himself, voted with the party majority more than three-quarters of the time.[12] The figures range from 96.4 per cent for Bayard to 77.2 per cent for Rice. Other senators voting with the Democratic majority less than 80 per cent of the time were Henderson (77.5 per cent) and McDougall (79.1 per cent). In addition to Bayard, four other senators voted with the party majority more than 90 per cent of the time—Nesmith (92.3 per cent), Latham (91.9 per cent), Saulsbury 91.8 per cent), and Stark (90.7 per cent).[13]

Despite the cooperativeness and sense of responsibility demonstrated by the Democrats, there were, of course, areas of disagreement with the Republicans. Generally speaking, the Democrats opposed emancipation (however accomplished), raising Negro troops, stringent confiscation legislation, and any confirmation of "illegal" presidential acts. There was, however, little effort to prevent Senate action even on these measures, though Bayard warned the Republicans less than a month after the first session began that any attempt to force bills dealing with military arrests and suspension of habeas corpus through the Senate without discussion would result in the use of parliamentary delaying tactics.

Though the dead spots in the Senate's legislative schedule were frequently filled with lengthy speeches (by members of all three political groups) having little bearing

on any legislation under consideration, the Democrats kept well within the bounds of legitimate debate. They often attacked the Republicans bitterly. They sponsored measures which narrowly defined the purpose of the war and sometimes called for negotiations with representatives of the seceded states. But their contributions were frequently constructive and their votes conclusively show that they were much more often a part of the senatorial consensus than might have been expected.

The Democratic strength in the lower house was concentrated in the delegations from New York, New Jersey, Pennsylvania, Ohio, Indiana, and Illinois. Thirty-seven of the forty-nine Democratic representatives came from these states. There were, in addition, three from New England, eight from the border states, and one from the West Coast. In the House of Representatives, more than in the Senate, individuals tend to be submerged, the institutional organization dominates, and small partisan minorities are cast into outer legislative darkness. Here, to be sure, the Democrats had had more experience with minority operations—they had controlled the House for only two of the last six years—but their total strength was now less than half what it had been in the Thirty-sixth Congress. They could expect scant consideration from the majority. But these were unusual times. The Republicans were already hard at work attempting to form a "Union" coalition. When the House committees were announced, five minor committee chairmanships went to Democrats; William Allen of Ohio, Jesse Lazear of Pennsylvania, John A. Logan of Illinois, Moses F. Odell of New York, and James C. Robinson of Illinois. Of these, Allen and Logan later became Republicans.

The House Democrats did not trouble

---

[12]Because of their limited service, the individual performances of Breckinridge, Waldo P. Johnson, Polk, Richardson, Turpie, and Wall were not analyzed. Andrew Johnson's unity factor was 42.6 per cent.

[13]Figures on the other senators were: Bright (88.9 per cent), Powell (88.5 per cent), Pearce (82.8 per cent), and Thomas (81 per cent).

themselves with the empty formality of making a caucus nomination for Speaker. Five of the minority members voted for Republican Francis P. Blair, Jr., of Missouri and the rest divided their votes among eight of their colleagues. John S. Phelps of Missouri and Clement L. Vallandigham of Ohio each received seven votes and Erastus Corning of New York and Samuel S. Cox of Ohio garnered six votes each. Three votes were cast for William A. Richardson of Illinois, two for John A. McClernand of Illinois, and one each for George H. Pendleton of Ohio and John W. Noell of Missouri.

It was from this group that one might have expected the Democratic House leadership to be drawn, but such was not the case. Indeed, no Democratic representative emerged as the recognized leader of the House minority, and any institutional organization was distinctly limited.

There were certainly no regular caucuses and none seem to have been held except during the spring of 1862 when the Democrats were looking to the forthcoming elections. The aim of the House Democrats was to produce a union of all anti-Republican forces under Democratic leadership. When some tentative steps in this direction in late March proved abortive, several of the Democrats decided to act independently. In early May a "Democratic Address" was issued which condemned the Republicans and declared that only the Democrats could successfully prosecute the war, reunite the nation, and preserve personal liberty. The border state Unionists, however, remained aloof and, apparently still hoping for a more potent coalition, a majority of the Democratic representatives declined to sign the "Address."[14] Addition-

al meetings in May and June, 1862, led to effective cooperation with the Unionists to block or modify Radical legislative proposals, but not to political amalgamation.[15]

But if the House Democrats were unwilling to institutionalize a union among themselves and were unable to establish a coalition party, it does not follow that there was, in fact, an absence of unity among the members of the House minority. On the contrary, an analysis of a sixty-nine-vote sample shows the Democrats casting unanimous votes almost 32 per cent of the time.[16] In more than 78 per cent of the instances, 80 per cent or more of the minority representatives voted together. On only five votes (7.2 per cent of the sample) did the Democratic unity factor fall below 60 per cent.[17] These figures show the House Democrats to be (except for a smaller percentage of unanimous votes) slightly more united than the Senate minority. This unity is reflected in other figures as well. More than 68 per cent of the House Democrats sided with the majority of their party at least 90 per cent of the time. Less than 15 per cent of the minority members failed to vote with the Democratic majority at least 80 per cent of the time. At one extreme, Sydenham E.

---

[14]Only fourteen Democratic representatives signed the "Address."

[15]The attendance at the May 10 caucus (the only one for which accurate figures are obtainable) included twenty-two Democrats (two of them senators), twenty Unionists (including one senator), and one Republican (Representative William Kellogg of Illinois).

[16]By comparison, it might be noted that the House Republicans were unanimous less than 15 per cent of the time. All subsequent observations regarding House voting are based on an analysis of this sixty-nine vote sample. The House sample is smaller than the Senate sample primarily because the operation of the "previous question" in the House frequently prevented the offering of amendments. Hence there are many fewer preliminary votes on any given measure.

[17]Less than 60 per cent of the Republicans voted together on 13 per cent of the votes.

Ancona and Philip Johnson of Pennsylvania, and Henry May of Maryland, never failed to side with the party majority and nine other Democrats were to be found with the majority more than 95 per cent of the time.[18] At the other end of the scale, only four minority representatives had a unity factor of less than 75 per cent; Noell (56.5 per cent), Edward Haight of New York (63 per cent), Isaac C. Delaplaine of New York (65 per cent), and William E. Lehman of Pennsylvania (71.7 per cent).

This unity was maintained on most of the major issues. Eighty per cent or more of the Democrats stood together on all the votes involving slavery and the Negro, confiscation, and presidential indemnification, and on 70 per cent of the financial votes. Only in the area of public land and public improvement legislation did this picture of Democratic unity blur; on these measures the Democratic unity factor never reached 80 per cent.[19]

Several factors caused Democratic opposition in the House to take more stringent and obstructionist forms than it did in the Senate. The House Republicans—both the membership and the leadership—were considerably more radical than their party colleagues in the Senate. Furthermore, the technique of the "previous question" was frequently used not only to halt or prohibit debate, but also to prevent the submission of amendments. The Republican House leadership obviously feared (and with good

reason) that its political ranks, none too strong even on major pieces of legislation, would not stand firm against the gradual modification of party measures by successive amendments.

It was at this time possible to conduct a House filibuster by entering and demanding roll calls on a succession of overlapping, dilatory, and procedural motions. In order to force an open debate and to have the opportunity to submit amendments, the Democrats were on several occasions, driven to this expedient. On February 12 and again on February 27, 1863, Democratic filibusters forced the House leadership to permit debate on proposals designed to make it practically impossible for successful civil and criminal actions to be brought against executive and military officers on issues arising from the use of military arrest and suspension of habeas corpus. On March 2, 1863, similar actions delayed and, had the Democrats desired, could have prevented the passage of a bill to reorganize the District of Columbia courts.[20] On February 23 and 24, 1863, two successive filibusters forced the opening of the Conscription Bill to both debate and amendment.

Probably the most successful case of Democratic House filibustering involved a bill to raise Negro troops which came before the House in late January, 1863. House Republican leader Thaddeus Stevens wished to have the bill passed without extensive debate, without amendment, and without reference to the Committee on Military Affairs (which had consistently refused to report such legislation). But on January 28, a group of predominantly Democratic representatives under the *ad hoc* leadership of Clement Vallandigham launched a most effective filibuster. Stevens

---

[18]The individual performances of the fourteen Democratic House members who served for only a portion of the Congress were not analyzed. An analysis was made of the records of each of the forty-one Democrats who served the full two years. All subsequent observations regarding individual performances of House members is based on this group analysis.

[19]This sixty-nine vote sample includes twenty-seven votes dealing with slavery and the Negro, ten financial votes, eight votes involving public lands and public improvements, four votes on confiscation measures, and four votes dealing with presidential indemnification.

---

[20] The main purpose of the bill was to legislate two judges out of office.

was deeply committed to the measure and the House leadership capitulated only after the filibusters had forced four calls of the House, thirty-nine roll call votes on adjournment and procedural motions, and kept the House in continuous session until 5:35 the following morning. In the four days of debate that followed, the measure underwent significant modification. Every change was a concession to the Democratic and Unionist opposition and the Negrophobe sentiments of many midwestern Republicans.

Most of the Democratic opposition, of course, was less spectacular. In numerous speeches the minority representatives attacked Lincoln, the Republican party, abolitionism, and the conduct of the war. Many of these indictments were (like speeches in a quite different vein delivered by the Republicans) obviously designed to be circulated as campaign documents. Democratic members were active in opposing stringent confiscation legislation, attempts to confirm "illegal" presidential acts, the use of Negro troops, the exchange of ministers with Haiti and Liberia, and practically all emancipation measures. Some Democrats also repeatedly urged conciliatory advances to the Confederate government.

Not all Democratic actions were of a negative nature, though they had even less chance than their colleagues in the Senate to play an affirmative role in the introduction and management of legislation. William S. Holman's resolution limiting House debate during the first session to military and financial matters decisively shaped the course of events during this session. Vallandigham fought for homestead legislation, Holman for land bounties for soldiers, and Elijah Ward of New York wrote a national bankruptcy bill which commanded wide support.[21] But, on the

whole, as would be expected, most of the legislation of the Thirty-seventh Congress was sponsored and managed by the Republicans.

That there was a considerable amount of Democratic opposition to these Republican measures was to be expected. But this opposition should not be allowed to obscure the broader picture of the mass of legislation on which the members of both parties were in general agreement. In the House, as in the Senate, civil and military appropriations bills and measures to strengthen and reorganize the army and navy were generally passed with little discussion and without a division, though Holman was already becoming noted for his determination to eradicate buried appropriations and to cut non-military expenditures.

The area of general agreement extended to non-war measures as well. On more than a third of the votes analyzed the Democratic majority formed a part of the House majority, and almost 16 per cent of the time the Democratic and Republican majorities stood together.[22] On issues connected with slavery and the Negro, a majority of the Democratic members were also found in the House majority almost a quarter of the time. The same conditions prevailed on 50 per cent of the financial votes,[23] 75 per cent of the votes involving public lands and public improvements, and a quarter of the presidential indemnification votes. Further, the Democratic and Republican majorities were allied on 20 per cent of the financial votes,[24] 50 per cent of the public land and public improvement votes, and on 25 per cent of the votes con-

---

[21]Holman was a representative from Indiana.

[22]Included is one vote on which there was no Democratic majority.

[23]Included is one vote on which the Democrats were evenly divided.

[24]Included is one vote on which there was no Democratic majority.

cerned with indemnification of presidential acts. The Democratic majority did not join with the Republicans in any case involving slavery and the Negro or confiscation legislation, nor did the Democratic majority form a part of the House majority on any of the confiscation votes.

The minority party also gave quite significant support to a number of measures considered to be Republican in nature. On February 20, 1862, 86.7 per cent of the Democrats and 81.9 per cent of the Republicans voted against tabling the Legal Tender Bill. A motion to postpone the Homestead Bill, in December, 1861, was opposed by a higher percentage of Democrats than Republicans, and 72 per cent of the minority members supported the Homestead Bill on the final vote. More than half of the House Democrats joined with the Republicans to prevent the reference of the Land Grant College Bill to a hostile committee, and almost 64 per cent of the minority members voted for the passage of the measure. More than 47 per cent of the Democrats even supported the bill to authorize the President to seize and operate railways and telegraph lines.

Obviously the House Democrats joined with the Republicans or formed a part of the general majority far less frequently than their party colleagues in the Senate. Several considerations can be advanced to explain this situation. The Republican representatives were, on the whole, considerably more radical by persuasion than their counterparts in the Senate, and the Republican leadership was far more radical in the lower house than in the upper. It can be further observed that the methods of legislative operation in the House were such as to make the majority members far more responsive to the leadership than was true in the Senate. Since there were no Radicals in the Democratic ranks, it was only natural that the minority members

should find themselves less often in agreement with the Radical House Republicans than with the more moderate Republican senators.

Another aspect of legislative operations helps to account for the different degrees of interparty harmony in the two houses. The Senate rules permitted almost unlimited submission of amendments, and it was on amendments, rather than on the bills themselves, that the two parties most frequently joined forces in the upper house. But through the use of the "previous question" the House leadership held the introduction of amendments to a bare minimum. A broad area of potential interparty cooperation was thus almost entirely eliminated from the House deliberations.

These observations suggest that the higher degree of cooperativeness exhibited by the Senate Democrats resulted not from any significant differences of opinion between the House and Senate Democrats, but, rather, from differences of opinion between the House and Senate Republicans. This conclusion is most assuredly correct. The Democrats in both houses, as has been pointed out, took almost identical stands on most of the major issues dealt with by this Congress. In the entire vote sample there are sixteen issues or measures which came before both houses either in the same or in highly comparable form. On only two issues did the House and Senate Democratic majorities split, and both of these measures—the Homestead Bill and the Pacific Railway Bill—tended to divide congressmen along geographic lines. On ten of the other fourteen issues the Democratic House and Senate unity factors varied by no more than ten percentage points.

It is obvious that the congressional Democrats had, by any method of measurement, a high degree of unity. Further, this unity was not achieved by institutional control. Nor can it be argued that the basis of this unity was geographic, for Democrats in the Thirty-seventh Congress represented thirteen states, stretching from Rhode Island to California. Nor can it be suggested that this unity was achieved only because secession had removed from the Congress all the "Administration" adherents in the party. For though there were more Douglasites among the representatives, the Democratic senators were, with only four exceptions, Breckinridge supporters. The only feasible explanation seems to be that there was, within Democratic party ranks, a common adherence to certain basic elements of political philosophy and practice which were far more deep-rooted and widespread than one normally expects to find in American political parties. Certainly there was within the Democratic party far greater uniformity of opinion than within the Republican party.

The frequency with which the Democrats supported "Republican" measures and voted with majorities or large minorities of the Republican membership conclusively demonstrates that they were not extremists. Indeed, except for a few aberrant individuals, it is clear that the congressional Democrats formed an integral and important part of the old political "center"— that massive repository of political power in America. Because the old "right" had been largely stripped away by secession, the Democratic remnant superficially appeared to be farther removed from the center than it actually was.[25] But this was no mid-nineteenth century "radical right." In attempting to assess the Democratic position one comes, by whatever road, even-

tually and almost inevitably to the word "conservative." The governmental philosophy they desired to "conserve" included the preservation of constitutional guarantees, both individual and corporate; the reestablishment of the Union by the time-honored method of compromise or, failing that, the reunification of the nation on the basis of mutual concession after a victorious army had destroyed the Confederacy; a scrupulous regard for property rights, including (and here they differed even from many of the most moderate Republicans) slave property rights; and a limited federal participation in the national life. These views they shared with most Unionists and with many moderate Republicans as well. Having sloughed off the remnants of their "radical left" during the years following 1852, and having lost their "radical right" in 1860–1861, the congressional Democrats were left with an unorganized, but relatively homogeneous, center.[26]

It is quite clear, then, that the congressional Democrats of these early Civil War years were thoroughly loyal to the Union, consistent in their support of the war effort, reasoned and responsible in their approach to non-war measures, possessed of a high degree of internal unity, and conservative in their political and economic orientation. All of which produces a rather different picture than might have been expected and a picture that differs radically from the traditional one.

---

[25] There is an apparent, but no real, contradiction between this assertion and the statement made in the previous paragraph. For many "Administration" supporters had not adhered to the philosophy of the "right." Hence, the "right" could be (and was) largely eliminated without removing all of the "Administration" faction.

[26] Slavery must, of course, be the touchstone of the "left" and "right" in the mid-nineteenth century context. The "radical left" had desired federal intervention to establish human freedom. The "radical right" had desired federal intervention to preserve human slavery. The "center" preferred a solution which would involve the federal government only minimally and which would eliminate periodic renewal of agitation, e.g., popular sovereignty. To this basically laissez faire approach, many mid-nineteenth century "liberals" and "conservatives" alike could adhere.

Guide for Further Reading

In spite of the outpouring of books on the American Civil War there is no scholarly synthesis of Civil War politics. There is no solid history of either major party during the war. And neither is there a historiographical article on politics and the Civil War, although historians have systematically surveyed the political historiography of the 1850s and of Reconstruction.

The explanation of these great gaps in American historical writing may lie in the overweening interest historians have taken in Abraham Lincoln, in military affairs, and in the dramatic conflict they have depicted between Lincoln and the Radical Republicans and between Unionists and Copperheads. Historians have made many fragmentary studies of politics, but these have tended to be not only episodic but also often sensational. A selective bibliography can be compiled only with a realization of these attributes of the period's political literature.

The great repository for the raw materials of Union politics is the *Congressional Globe* during the years 1861–1865. Here are the debates of the national lawmakers of both parties, their votes, the fugitive materials inserted at congressmen's request, and the lists of members for each session. A compact distillation of the *Globe*, by the clerk of the House of Representatives, is Edward McPherson, *Political History of the United States during the Rebellion*. Of great importance is Roy P. Basler *et al.* (eds.), *The Collected Works of Abraham Lincoln* (9 vols.; New Brunswick, N.J., 1953–1955).

Several published diaries illuminate the inner history of wartime politics. Lincoln's secretary, John Hay, kept perhaps the best of Civil War diaries: Tyler Dennett (ed.), *Lincoln and the Civil War in the Diaries and Letters of John Hay* (New York, 1939). Three cabinet members

kept diaries: Howard K. Beale (ed.), *The Diary of Edward Bates, 1859–1866* (Washington, 1933); David Donald (ed.), *Inside Lincoln's Cabinet: The Civil War Diaries of Salmon P. Chase* (New York, 1954); and Howard K. Beale (ed.), *Diary of Gideon Welles, Secretary of the Navy under Lincoln and Johnson* (3 vols.; New York, 1960). These editions of the Chase and Welles diaries supplant earlier inaccurate versions and are superbly edited. The Illinois senator, and friend of Lincoln, Orville H. Browning, maintained a diary: Theodore C. Pease and James G. Randall (eds.), *The Diary of Orville Hickman Browning* (2 vols.; Springfield, Ill., 1927, 1933). The Polish count Adam Gurowski, described as "Lincoln's Gadfly," wrote an acidulous *Diary* (3 vols.; Boston, New York, and Washington, 1862–1866).

Leonard P. Curry, *Blueprint for Modern America: Nonmilitary Legislation of the First Civil War Congress* (Nashville, Tenn., 1968) is a splendid beginning to a greatly needed history of Congress during the war.

The two magisterial histories of the era of the Civil War give much attention to politics. Volumes 3 to 5 of James Ford Rhodes, *History of the United States from the Compromise of 1850 [to 1877]* (7 vols.; New York, 1893–1906), represented at the time of publication a scholarly advance in impartiality and thoroughness. Rhodes is being superseded by Allan Nevins, whose *The War for the Union* (2 vols.; New York, 1959, 1960), carries the narrative to the spring of 1863. A work widely used in colleges is James G. Randall and David Donald, *The Civil War and Reconstruction*, (2d ed. rev.; Boston, 1969), which contains two chapters and more and an excellent bibliography on wartime politics.

Modern party historians who moved away from traditional stress on rival constitutional principles include Wilfred E. Binkley and Herbert Agar. The former essayed a "natural history" of group combinations practicing the art of group diplomacy in his *American Political Parties* (New York, 1945); and Agar unfolded his thesis that through parties rival interests find grounds for compromise in *The Price of Union* (Boston, 1950). A good general history is George H. Mayer, *The Republican Party, 1854–1966* (New York, 1967). James A. Rawley, *Edwin D. Morgan, 1811–1883* (New York, 1955) is a life of the first Republican national chairman based on the hitherto unused Morgan papers. The role of the Democrats during the war remains shrouded in partisanship; there is, however, a superlatively objective analysis of the party in the 1850s by Roy F. Nichols: *The Disruption of American Democracy* (New York, 1948).

Scholarly biographies of Lincoln are James G. Randall, *Lincoln the President* (4 vols.; New York, 1945–1955), the final volume written in collaboration with Richard N. Current, a great authority who felt sympathy for the Democrats and the Confederacy; Benjamin Thomas, *Abraham Lincoln* (New York, 1952), the best single-volume life. For Lincoln and the Constitution the student may consult James G. Randall, *Constitutional Problems Under Lincoln* (rev. ed.; Urbana, Ill., 1951) and his "Lincoln in the Role of Dictator," *South Atlantic Quarterly*, XXVIII (July, 1929), 236–252. Albert V. Dicey, *Introduction to the Study of the Law of the Constitution* (7th ed.; London, 1908) explains, in Chapter 4, the English conception of the "rule of law." Horace Binney, *The Privilege of the Writ of Habeas Corpus under the Constitution* (Philadelphia, 1862) is a learned contemporary defense of suspension of the writ. Alfred H. Kelly and Winfred E. Harbison ably cover the Civil War period in *The American Constitution* (New York, 1948). Carl B. Swisher, in *Roger B. Taney* (New York, 1935), relates the life of the chief justice of the Supreme Court critical of Lincoln for lack of adherence to constitutional principles. David M. Silver, *Lincoln's Supreme Court* (Urbana, Ill., 1956) is a scholarly analysis.

A pioneer account is Carl R. Fish, "Lincoln and the Patronage," *American Historical Review*, VIII (October, 1902), 53–69. William B. Hesseltine's presentation of the President's relations with the state executives did not pass unchallenged; see the review by R. H. Luthin, *American Historical Review*, LIV (July, 1949), 887–889. Biographies of outstanding war governors include William D. Foulke, *Life of Oliver P. Morton* (2 vols.; Indianapolis, Ind., 1899); Henry G. Pearson, *The Life of John A. Andrew, Governor of Massachusetts, 1861–1865* (Boston, 1904); Rawley, *Morgan,* cited above; and Stewart Mitchell, *Horatio Seymour of New York* (Cambridge, 1938), the so-called Copperhead governor who held office at the time of the New York City draft riots.

Wilfred E. Binkley, *President and Congress* (New York, 1947) contains a perceptive study. Two accounts by leading congressmen are: James G. Blaine, *Twenty Years of Congress* (2 vols.; Norwich, Conn., 1884–1886) and John Sherman, *John Sherman's Recollections of Forty Years in the House, Senate and Cabinet: an Autobiography* (2 vols.; Chicago, 1896). After Douglas's death in 1861 the northern Democrats were left without a leader; for the emergence of General McClellan as a politician and his 1864 candidacy, see William S. Meyers, *A Study in Personality, General George Brinton McClellan* (New York, 1934) and H. J. Eckenrode and Bryan Conrad, *George B. McClellan: The Man Who Saved the Union* (Chapel Hill, N.C., 1941).

The fountainhead of material on the principal Radical agency is *Report of the Joint Committee on the Conduct of the War* (8 vols.; Washington, 1863–1866). An early balanced study is William W. Pierson, Jr., "The Committee on the Conduct of the War," *American Historical Review*, XXIII (April, 1918), 550–576. After T. Harry Williams presented his revisionist view, in *Lincoln and the Radicals* (Madison, Wis., 1941), David Donald challenged him, arguing that Lincoln and the Radicals were substantially in agreement; see *Lincoln Reconsidered* (Vintage edition; New York, 1961), Chapter 4. Williams and Donald continued their debate, refining their argument, in Grady McWhiney (ed.), *Grant, Lee, Lincoln and the Radicals* (Evanston, Ill., 1964), pp. 72–117.

Biographies of leading Radicals include Fawn N. Brodie, *Thaddeus Stevens: Scourge of the South* (New York, 1959); Edward L. Pierce, *Memoir and Letters of Charles Sumner* (4 vols.; Boston, 1887–1893); Hans L. Trefousse, *Benjamin Franklin Wade* (New York, 1963); and no author given, *Zachariah Chandler* (Detroit, 1880). William D. Mallam, in "Lincoln and the Conservatives," *Journal of Southern History*, XXXVIII (February, 1962), 31–45, attempts to overturn the conception of Lincoln standing alone in the defense and implementation of his policies, defeated at every turn by the Radicals.

With quantification historical research has found a new dimension. A good brief introduction to the advantages and shortcomings of the quantitative method is William O. Aydelotte, "Quantification in History," *American Historical Review*, LXXI (April, 1966), 803–825. On the Guttman-scale technique, see George M. Belnap, "A Method for Analyzing Legislative Behavior," *Midwest Journal of Political Science*, II (November, 1958), 377–402. Explanations of key aspects of quantification may be found in Lee F. Anderson *et al.*, *Legislative Roll-Call Analysis* (Evanston, Ill., 1966), pp. 59–73 for cluster-bloc analysis, pp. 35–40 for indexes of cohesion, and pp. 89–121 for Guttman-scale analysis.

Although historical literature on the Copperheads abounds, it needs a new synthesis. Two early studies are: Elbert J. Benton, *The Movement for Peace Without Victory* (Cleveland, 1909) and Mayo Fesler, "Secret Political Societies in the North during the Civil War," *Indiana Magazine of History*, XIV (September, 1918), 183–286; both offer traditional views. An able popular account comprehending the entire North is George Fort Milton, *Abraham Lincoln and the Fifth Column* (New York, 1930). Wood Gray, *The Hidden Civil War: The Story of the Copperheads* (New York, 1964) rests on more thoroughgoing scholarship and is the standard study, portraying Middle Western Copperheads as lacking in realism and, in cases, in loyalty. A revisionist view of the movement in the Middle West is Frank Klement, *The Copperheads in the Middle West* (Chicago, 1960), which identifies the Copperheads as the loyal opposition, although partisan, and Januslike looking backward to Jeffersonian-Jacksonian agrarianism and forward to Grangerism. A perceptive recent essay is William G. Carleton, "Civil War Dissidence in the North: The Perspective of a Century," *South Atlantic Quarterly*, LXV (Summer, 1966), 390–402.

The early rise of vitriolic politics during the war is noted in Charles H. Coleman, "The Use of the Term 'Copperhead' during the Civil War," *Mississippi Valley Historical Review*, XXV (September, 1938), 263–264. Antagonism toward abolitionists and Negroes is the theme of Ray H. Abrams, "Copperhead Newspapers and the Negro," *Journal of Negro History*, XX (April, 1935), 131–152. Studies of Copperheadism in individual states include Kenneth Stampp, *Indiana Politics during the Civil War* (Indianapolis, Ind., 1949), which essays to rehabilitate the Hoosier Democrats, and Eugene H. Rosebloom, "Southern Ohio and the Union in 1863," *Mississippi Valley Historical Review*, XXXIX (June, 1952), 29–44, which denies the charge of Elbert Benton and other writers that the region was a stronghold of the Peace Democrats.

A biography of the mayor of New York City who recommended that the city secede is Samuel A. Pleasants, *Fernando Wood of New York* (New York, 1949). The situation in another major eastern city is analyzed in Nicholas B. Wainwright, "The Loyal Opposition in Civil War Philadelphia," *Pennsylvania Magazine of History and Biography*, LXXX (July, 1964), 294–315.

The most notorious Copperhead may be studied in James L. Vallandigham, *A Life of Clement L. Vallandigham* (Baltimore, 1872), Clement L. Vallandigham, *Speeches, Arguments, Addresses, and Letters* (New York, 1864), and *The Trial of Hon. Clement L. Vallandigham, by a Military Commission: and the Proceedings under His Application for a Writ of Habeas Corpus in the Circuit Court of the United States for the Southern District of Ohio* (Cincinnati, 1863).

Charles R. Wilson revealed "McClellan's Changing Views on the Peace Plank of 1864," in *American Historical Review*, XXXVIII (April, 1933), 498–505. Dissension in Republican ranks in 1864 is the theme of William F. Zornow, *Lincoln and the Party Divided* (Norman, Okla., 1954). James A. Rawley suggests an opposing view of the election and interprets other political themes in *Turning Points of the Civil War* (Lincoln, Neb., 1965).

Northern anti-Negro prejudice, although underscored in the 1830s by Alexis de Tocqueville

in *Democracy in America,* only recently came under clinical investigation. Leon Litwack, in
North of Slavery (Chicago, 1961), surveys bias in
the free states from 1790 to 1860; and Eugene
H. Berwanger, in *The Frontier Against Slavery*
(Urbana, Ill., 1967), examines western bias in
connection with the slavery extension controversy.

Schemes to deport Negroes are discussed in:
Walter L. Fleming, "Deportation and Coloni-
zation: An Attempted Solution of the Race
Problem," J. G. de Roulhac Hamilton (ed.),
*Studies in Southern History and Politics Inscribed to
William Archibald Dunning* (New York, 1914);
Warren A. Beck, "Lincoln and Negro Coloni-
zation in Central America," *Abraham Lincoln
Quarterly,* VI (September, 1950), 162–183; and
Frederic Bancroft, "The Colonization of Ameri-

can Negroes, 1810–1865," Jacob E. Cooke
(ed.), *Frederic Bancroft, Historian* (Norman, Okla.,
1957). Jacque Voegeli has extended his study of
midwestern attitudes toward the Negro
throughout the Civil War in *Free But Not Equal*
(Chicago, 1967).

New directions in scholarship on the Copperheads are discussed in Richard O. Curry's distin-
guished essay "The Union As It Was: A Critique
of Recent Interpretations of the 'Copperheads,'" *Civil War History,* XIII (March, 1967),
25–39.

The student who wishes to keep informed
of the continuing dialogue among historians
about Lincoln and Civil War politics should
consult the annual bibliography of Civil War
literature published by *Civil War History* (Kent,
Ohio).